# Rick Steves®

# POCKET

# LONDON

Rick Steves & Gene Openshaw

# Contents

# Introduction

Blow through the city on a double-decker bus, and wander the lively West End. Hear the chimes of Big Ben, ogle the crown jewels at the Tower of London, and go for a spin on the London Eye. Visit with Van Gogh in the National Gallery, and rummage through our civilization's attic at the British Museum. Top off your day tipping a pint in a pub with a chatty local.

This is London. It's a city that seems perpetually at your service, with an impressive slate of sights, entertainment, and eateries, all linked by a great transit system. With a growing number of immigrants from all over the world, London has become a city of 10 million separate dreams, learning—sometimes fitfully—to live as a microcosm of the once-vast British Empire.

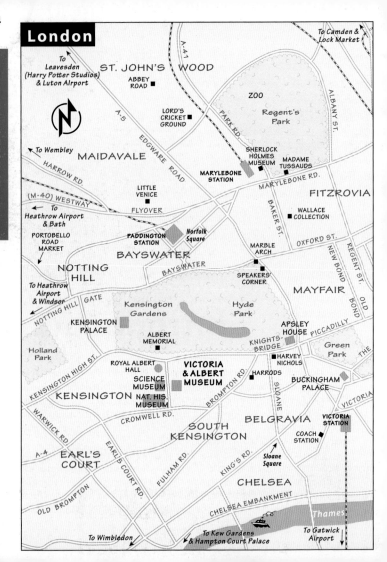

# London

St. John's Wood
To Camden & Lock Market
To Leavesden (Harry Potter Studios) & Luton Airport
Abbey Road
Lord's Cricket Ground
Zoo
Regent's Park
Albany St.
Park Rd.
To Wembley
Maidavale
Harrow Rd.
Edgware Road
A-5
A-41
Sherlock Holmes Museum
Madame Tussauds
Marylebone Station
Marylebone Rd.
Fitzrovia
(M-40) Westway
Little Venice
Baker St.
Wallace Collection
To Heathrow Airport & Bath
Flyover
Portobello Road Market
Paddington Station
Norfolk Square
Bayswater
Marble Arch
Oxford St.
New Bond St.
Regent St.
Old Bond St.
Notting Hill
Bayswater
Speakers Corner
Mayfair
To Heathrow Airport & Windsor
Notting Hill Gate
Kensington Gardens
Hyde Park
Apsley House
Piccadilly
Green Park
The
Holland Park
Kensington Palace
Albert Memorial
Knightsbridge
Harvey Nichols
Kensington High St.
Royal Albert Hall
Victoria & Albert Museum
Harrods
Buckingham Palace
Science Museum
Nat. His. Museum
Brompton Rd.
Sloane St.
Victoria
Kensington
Cromwell Rd.
Belgravia
Victoria Station
Warwick Rd.
South Kensington
Coach Station
Earl's Court
Earls Court Rd.
Fulham Rd.
King's Rd.
Sloane Square
Old Brompton
A-4
Chelsea
To Wimbledon
Chelsea Embankment
Thames
To Kew Gardens & Hampton Court Palace
To Gatwick Airport

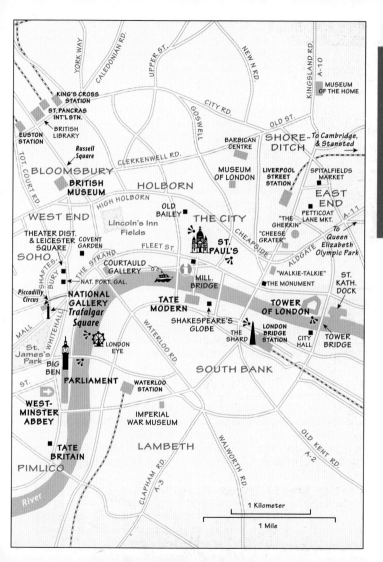

## About This Book

*Rick Steves Pocket London* is a personal tour guide...in your pocket. The core of the book is seven self-guided tours. These zero in on London's greatest sights, from a Westminster Walk past #10 Downing Street, to the treasures of the British Library, to the glittering crown jewels at the Tower of London.

The rest of this book is a traveler's tool kit, with my best advice on how to save money, plan your time, ride public transportation, and avoid lines at the busiest sights. You'll also get recommendations on hotels, restaurants, and activities.

## London by Neighborhood

London, with more than 600 square miles and 10 million people, is a world in itself. On my first visit, I felt extremely small. But when you consider it as a collection of neighborhoods, London becomes manageable.

The River Thames runs roughly west to east through the city, with most sights on the North Bank (in the area roughly enclosed by the Tube's Circle Line).

**Central London:** The heart of today's London contains the Westminster district (Big Ben, the Abbey, and Parliament) and the West End (Piccadilly Circus, theaters, restaurants, and nightlife). In the middle sits London's gathering place, Trafalgar Square.

**North London:** This contains the British Museum, the British Library, the overhyped Madame Tussauds Waxworks, and three major train stations.

**The City:** Surrounding St. Paul's Cathedral is the former walled city of Shakespeare's day. Now it's the modern financial district, called simply "The City." On its eastern border stands the Tower of London.

**East London:** East of The City is the once-grimy, increasingly gentrified East End.

**The South Bank:** The Thames' South Bank offers major sights (Shakespeare's Globe, Tate Modern, London Eye) and minor attractions, all linked by a riverside walkway.

**West London:** This huge area surrounding the green expanse of Hyde Park/Kensington Gardens contains upscale neighborhoods such as Mayfair, Belgravia, Chelsea, South Kensington, and Notting Hill. Here you'll find a range of sights (Victoria and Albert Museum, Tate Britain, Harrods) and my top hotel recommendations.

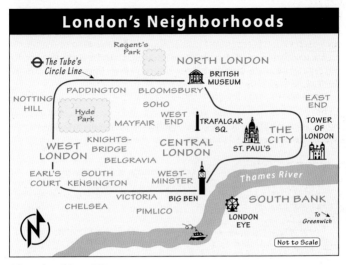

## London's Neighborhoods

## Planning Your Time

The following day-plans give an idea of how much an organized, motivated, and caffeinated person can see. You won't be able to see everything, so don't try. You'll keep coming back to London. After dozens of visits myself, I still enjoy a healthy list of excuses to return.

**Day 1:** Use my Westminster Walk to link the following sights: Start at Westminster Abbey at opening for fewer crowds, then visit the Churchill War Rooms and have lunch. Visit the National Gallery and nearby sights that interest you. Have a pub dinner before a play, concert, or evening walking tour.

**Day 2:** Take a London sightseeing bus tour and hop off at Buckingham Palace for the Changing of the Guard. After lunch, tour the British Museum and/or the British Library. Do some evening shopping at one of London's elegant department stores.

**Day 3:** Visit the Tower of London, then have a picnic lunch on the Thames while cruising to Blackfriars Pier. Tour St. Paul's Cathedral and climb its dome for views. Walk across Millennium Bridge to the South Bank to visit the Tate Modern, Shakespeare's Globe Theatre, or other sights. Catch a play at the Globe.

**With More Time:** Choose from other major sights: Victoria

## London at a Glance

▲▲▲**Westminster Abbey** Britain's finest church and the site of royal coronations and burials since 1066. **Hours:** Abbey—Mon-Fri 9:30-16:30, Wed until 19:00, Sat 9:00-16:00 (Sept-April until 14:00); Diamond Jubilee Galleries—Mon-Fri 10:00-16:00, Sat 9:30-15:30; closed Sun except for worship. See page 27.

▲▲▲**Churchill War Rooms** Underground WWII headquarters of Churchill's war effort. **Hours:** Daily 9:30-18:00, July-Aug until 19:00. See page 124.

▲▲▲**National Gallery** Remarkable collection of European paintings (1250-1900), including Leonardo, Botticelli, Velázquez, Rembrandt, Turner, Van Gogh, and the Impressionists. **Hours:** Daily 10:00-18:00, Fri until 21:00. See page 41.

▲▲▲**British Museum** The world's greatest collection of artifacts of Western civilization, including the Rosetta Stone and the Parthenon's Elgin Marbles. **Hours:** Daily 10:00-17:30, Fri until 20:30 (select galleries only). See page 73.

▲▲▲**British Library** Fascinating collection of important literary treasures of the Western world. **Hours:** Mon-Thu 9:30-20:00, Fri until 18:00, Sat until 17:00, Sun 11:00-17:00. See page 97.

▲▲▲**St. Paul's Cathedral** The main cathedral of the Anglican Church, designed by Christopher Wren, with a climbable dome and daily evensong services. **Hours:** Mon-Sat 8:30-16:30, closed Sun except for worship. See page 138.

▲▲▲**Tower of London** Historic castle, palace, and prison housing the crown jewels and a witty band of Beefeaters. **Hours:** Tue-Sat 9:00-17:30, Sun-Mon from 10:00; Nov-Feb closes one hour earlier. See page 109.

▲▲▲**Victoria and Albert Museum** The best collection of decorative arts anywhere. **Hours:** Daily 10:00-17:45, Fri until 22:00 (select galleries only). See page 151.

▲▲**Houses of Parliament** Famous for Big Ben and occupied by the Houses of Lords and Commons. **Hours:** When Parliament is in session, generally open Oct-late July Mon-Thu, closed Fri-Sun and during recess late July-Sept. Guided tours offered year-round on Sat and most weekdays during recess. See page 122.

▲▲**Trafalgar Square** The heart of London, where Westminster, The City, and the West End meet. See page 24.

▲▲**National Portrait Gallery** A *Who's Who* of British history, featuring portraits of this nation's most important historical figures. **Hours:** Daily 10:00-18:00, Fri until 21:00. See page 126.

▲▲**Covent Garden** Vibrant people-watching zone with shops, cafés, street musicians, and an iron-and-glass arcade that once hosted a produce market. See page 65.

▲▲**Changing of the Guard at Buckingham Palace** Hour-long spectacle at Britain's royal residence. **Hours:** May-July daily at 11:00, Aug-April Sun-Mon, Wed, and Fri. See page 131.

▲▲**London Eye** Enormous observation wheel, dominating—and offering commanding views over—London's skyline. **Hours:** Daily 10:00-20:30 or later, Sept-May 11:00-18:00. See page 143.

▲▲**Imperial War Museum** Exhibits examining military conflicts from the early 20th century to today. **Hours:** Daily 10:00-18:00. See page 143.

▲▲**Tate Modern** Works by Monet, Matisse, Dalí, Picasso, and Warhol displayed in a converted powerhouse complex. **Hours:** Daily 10:00-18:00, Fri-Sat until 22:00. See page 144.

▲▲**Shakespeare's Globe** Timbered, thatched-roof reconstruction of the Bard's original "wooden O." **Hours:** Theater complex, museum, and actor-led tours generally daily 9:00-17:30; April-Oct generally morning theater tours only. Plays are also staged here. See page 146.

▲▲**Tate Britain** Collection of British painting from the 16th century through modern times, including works by Blake, the Pre-Raphaelites, and Turner. **Hours:** Daily 10:00-18:00. See page 149.

▲▲**Natural History Museum** A Darwinian delight, packed with stuffed creatures, engaging exhibits, and enthralled kids. **Hours:** Daily 10:00-18:00. See page 152.

▲▲**Greenwich** Seafaring borough just east of the city center, with *Cutty Sark* tea clipper, Royal Observatory, other maritime sights, and a pleasant market. **Hours:** Most sights open daily 10:00-17:00. See page 153.

## 🎧 Stick This Guidebook in Your Ear!

My free Rick Steves Audio Europe app makes it easy to download my audio tours of many of Europe's top attractions. In this book, this includes my Westminster Walk and tours of the British Museum, British Library, and St. Paul's Cathedral. Sights covered by audio tours are marked in the book with this symbol: 🎧. It's all free! For more info, see RickSteves.com/AudioEurope.

and Albert Museum, and/or its neighboring museums, Tate Britain, Museum of London, Imperial War Museum, or Kew Gardens. Explore a morning street market, stroll through Hyde Park, or consider a day trip outside the city.

## When to Go

July and August are peak season—my favorite time—with long days, the best weather, and the busiest schedule of tourist fun. Still, travelers during "shoulder season" (spring and fall) enjoy lower prices, smaller crowds, decent weather, and the full range of sights and tourist fun spots. London's sights are more crowded on three-day weekends, especially Bank Holidays on the first and last Mondays in May, and the last Monday in August.

Winter travelers find fewer crowds and soft room prices, but shorter sightseeing hours. The weather can be cold and dreary, and nightfall draws the shades on sightseeing well before dinnertime. While England's rural charm falls with the leaves, London sightseeing is fine in the winter, and is especially popular during the Christmas season.

## Before You Go

You'll have a smoother trip if you tackle a few things ahead of time. For more information on these topics, see the Practicalities chapter (and www.ricksteves.com, which has helpful travel tips and talks).

**Make sure your travel documents are valid.** If your passport is due to expire within six months of your ticketed date of return, you need to renew it. Allow up to six weeks to renew or get a passport

(www.travel.state.gov). While Britain is scheduled to leave the EU, it's uncertain how a "Brexit" might affect travelers.

**Arrange your transportation.** Book your international flights. If you're traveling beyond London, research rail passes, train reservations, and car rentals.

**Book rooms well in advance,** especially if your trip falls during peak season or any major holidays or festivals.

**Make reservations or buy tickets in advance for major sights or shows.** For simplicity, I **book plays** while in London (but if you have your heart set on a hot show, buying tickets in advance is safer). For the current schedule, visit www.officiallondontheatre.co.uk.

Prepurchasing tickets online can often save you about 10 percent on ticket prices—and a wait in the ticket-buying line—at the **Churchill War Rooms, Westminster Abbey, Houses of Parliament, St. Paul's Cathedral, Tower of London, London Eye,** and **Windsor Castle.**

**Consider travel insurance.** Compare the cost of the insurance to the cost of your potential loss. Check whether your existing insurance (health, homeowners, or renters) covers you and your possessions overseas.

**Call your bank.** Alert your bank that you'll be using your debit and credit cards in Europe. Ask about transaction fees, and get the PIN number for your credit card. You don't need to bring pounds for your trip; you can withdraw pounds from cash machines on arrival.

**Use your smartphone smartly.** Sign up for an international service plan to reduce your costs, or rely on Wi-Fi in Europe instead. Download any apps you'll want on the road, such as maps, translators, transit schedules, and Rick Steves Audio Europe (see sidebar).

**Pack light.** You'll walk with your luggage more than you think. I travel for weeks with a single carry-on bag and a daypack. Use the packing checklist later in this book as a guide.

# Westminster Walk

*From Big Ben to Trafalgar Square*

Just about every visitor to London strolls along historic Whitehall from Big Ben to Trafalgar Square. You'll get a whirlwind tour as well as a practical orientation to London. This quick nine-stop walk gives meaning to that touristy ramble.

As London's political center, the Westminster neighborhood is both historic and contemporary. See the Thames River, where London was born. Pass statues and monuments to the nation's great heroes. Admire the Halls of Parliament where Britain is ruled today, and take a peek at #10 Downing Street, home of the prime minister.

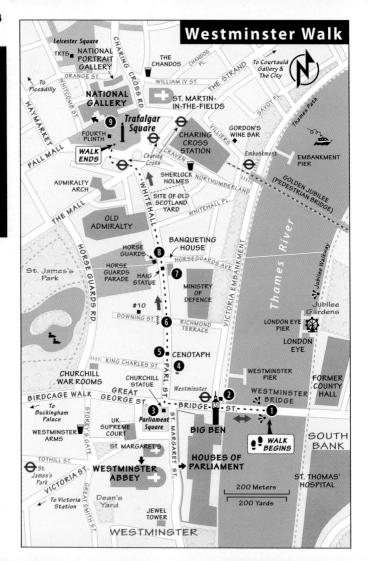

# Westminster Walk

Leicester Square
TKT9
CHARING CROSS RD.
NATIONAL PORTRAIT GALLERY
THE CHANDOS
CHANDOS PL.
WESTMINSTER
WILLIAM IV ST.
THE STRAND
To Courtauld Gallery & The City
ORANGE ST.
WHITCOMB ST.
To Piccadilly
HAYMARKET
NATIONAL GALLERY
ST. MARTIN-IN-THE-FIELDS
Savoy Pl.
Thames Path
9 Trafalgar Square
FOURTH PLINTH
GORDON'S WINE BAR
VILLIERS
CHARING CROSS STATION
WALK ENDS
Charing Cross
Embankment
EMBANKMENT PIER
CRAVEN
SHERLOCK HOLMES
NORTHUMBERLAND
GOLDEN JUBILEE (PEDESTRIAN BRIDGE)
PALL MALL
ADMIRALTY ARCH
WHITEHALL
SITE OF OLD SCOTLAND YARD
WHITEHALL PL.
THE MALL
OLD ADMIRALTY
Thames River
BANQUETING HOUSE
VICTORIA EMBANKMENT
HORSE GUARDS 8
HORSEGUARDS AVE.
Jubilee Walkway
St. James's Park
HORSE GUARDS PARADE
HAIG STATUE
7
MINISTRY OF DEFENCE
Jubilee Gardens
HORSE GUARDS RD.
#10 DOWNING ST.
6
RICHMOND TERRACE
LONDON EYE PIER
LONDON EYE
5 CENOTAPH
4
PARL. ST.
CHURCHILL WAR ROOMS
CHURCHILL STATUE
KING CHARLES ST.
Westminster
WESTMINSTER PIER
FORMER COUNTY HALL
BIRDCAGE WALK
GREAT GEORGE ST.
WESTMINSTER BRIDGE
To Buckingham Palace
WESTMINSTER ARMS
STOREY'S GATE
UK SUPREME COURT
3 Parliament Square
BRIDGE ST.
2
BIG BEN
1
WALK BEGINS
SOUTH BANK
TOTHILL ST.
St. James's Park
VICTORIA ST.
ST. MARGARET'S
ST. MARGARET ST.
GREAT SMITH ST.
WESTMINSTER ABBEY
HOUSES OF PARLIAMENT
To Victoria Station
Dean's Yard
JEWEL TOWER
200 Meters
200 Yards
ST. THOMAS' HOSPITAL
WESTMINSTER

# ORIENTATION

**Length of This Walk:** Though the walk itself only takes an hour, you'll need more time if you decide to go inside sights along the way.

**Getting There:** Take the Tube to Westminster, then take the Westminster Pier exit.

**Tours:** ∩ Download my free Westminster Walk audio tour.

**Services:** WCs along this walk are at Westminster Pier (pay), in Supreme Court (free), at the intersection of Bridge Street and Whitehall (underground, pay), and at Trafalgar Square (free, in square, at National Gallery, and downstairs at St. Martin-in-the-Fields).

**Eateries:** See page 184 for recommendations near Trafalgar Square, and page 28 for places near Westminster Abbey.

# THE WALK BEGINS

▶ *Start halfway across Westminster Bridge. Look upstream, toward Parliament.*

## ❶ Westminster Bridge

**Views of Big Ben and Parliament:** *Ding dong ding dong. Dong ding ding dong.* Yes, indeed, you are in London. Big Ben is actually "not the clock, not the tower, but the bell that tolls the hour." However, since the 13-ton bell is not visible, everyone just calls the whole works Big Ben. Named for a fat bureaucrat, Ben is scarcely older than my great-grandmother, but it has quickly become the city's symbol. The tower—officially named the "Elizabeth Tower" in honor of Queen Elizabeth II's Diamond Jubilee—is 315 feet high. The clock faces are 23 feet across, and the 13-foot-long minute hand sweeps the length of your body every five minutes. For fun, call home from near Big Ben at about three minutes before the hour to

| | |
|---|---|
| ❶ Westminster Bridge | ❻ #10 Downing Street & Ministry of Defence |
| ❷ Statue of Boadicea | |
| ❸ Parliament Square | ❼ Banqueting House |
| ❹ Walking Along Whitehall | ❽ Horse Guards |
| ❺ Cenotaph | ❾ Trafalgar Square |

let your loved one hear the bell ring. (If the bell is silent and scaffolding obscures some of the tower during your visit, it's due to a multiyear renovation of the tower and clock mechanism.)

Big Ben hangs out in the north tower of the Houses of Parliament (still known to Brits as the "Palace of Westminster"), which stretches along the Thames. Britain is ruled from this long building, which for five centuries was the home of kings and queens. Then, as democracy was foisted on tyrants, a parliament of nobles was allowed to meet in some of the rooms. Soon, commoners were elected to office, the neighborhood was shot, and the royalty moved to Buckingham Palace. While most of the current building looks medieval with its prickly flamboyant spires, it was actually reconstructed in the "Neo-Gothic" style after an 1834 fire destroyed the palace (which itself had been rebuilt following a fire in 1512).

Today, the House of Commons meets in one end of the building. The House of Lords debates and advises in the other end of this 1,000-room complex, providing a tempering effect on extreme governmental changes. The two houses are very much separate: Notice the riverside tea terraces with the color-coded awnings—royal red for lords, common green for commoners. The modern Portcullis Building (with the black tube-like chimneys), across Bridge Street from Big Ben, holds offices for many of the 650 members of the House of Commons. They commute to the Houses of Parliament by way of an underground passage.

▶ *Now look north (downstream).*

**The Thames:** London's history is tied to the Thames, the 210-mile river linking the interior of England with the North Sea. The city got its start in Roman times as a trade center along this watery highway. As recently as a century ago, large ships made their way upstream

Big Ben—the clock faces are 23 feet across.

The Thames snakes through London to the sea.

The London Eye—built to celebrate the Millennium—proved so popular, they decided to keep it.

to the city center to unload. Today, the major port is 25 miles downstream, and tourist cruise boats ply the waters.

Several tour-boat companies offer regular cruises from Westminster Pier (on the left) or London Eye Pier (on the right). This is an efficient, scenic way to get from here to the Tower of London or Greenwich (downstream) or Kew Gardens (upstream).

Until 1750, only London Bridge crossed the Thames. Then a bridge was built here. Early in the morning of September 3, 1802, William Wordsworth stood where you're standing and described what he saw:

*This City now doth, like a garment, wear*
*The beauty of the morning; silent, bare,*
*Ships, towers, domes, theatres, and temples lie*
*Open unto the fields, and to the sky;*
*All bright and glittering in the smokeless air.*

Across the river, on the South Bank, is the **London Eye**. This 443-foot-tall Ferris wheel—originally nicknamed "the London

Eyesore"—is now generally appreciated by locals, who see it as a welcome addition to their city's otherwise underwhelming skyline. Next to the wheel sprawls a carnival-like tourist complex. The London Eye marks the start of the Jubilee Walkway, a pleasant one-hour promenade along the vibrant, gentrified South Bank, with great views across the river.

▶ *Near Westminster Pier is a big statue of a lady on a chariot (nicknamed "the first woman driver"...no reins).*

## ❷ Statue of Boadicea, Queen of the Iceni

Riding in her two-horse chariot, daughters by her side, this Celtic Wonder Woman leads her people against Roman invaders. Julius Caesar was the first Roman general to cross the Channel, but even he was weirded out by the island's strange inhabitants, who worshipped trees, sacrificed virgins, and went to war painted blue. Later, Romans would subdue and civilize them, naming this spot on the Thames "Londinium" and building roads that turned it into a major urban center.

But Boadicea refused to be Romanized. In AD 60, after Roman soldiers raped her daughters, she rallied her people and "liberated" London, massacring its 60,000 Romanized citizens. However, the brief revolt was snuffed out, and she and her family took poison to avoid surrender.

▶ *Cross the street to just under Big Ben and continue one block inland to the busy intersection of Parliament Square.*

## ❸ Parliament Square

Admire the vast length of the sandstone-hued **Houses of Parliament.** If Parliament is in session, the entrance (midway down the building) is likely lined with tourists, enlivened by political demonstrations, and staked out by camera crews interviewing Members of Parliament (MPs) for the evening news.

Across the square, the two white towers of **Westminster Abbey** rise above the trees. The cute little church with the blue sundials, snuggling under the Abbey "like a baby lamb under a ewe," is **St. Margaret's Church.** Since 1480, this has been *the* place for politicians' weddings, including Winston and Clementine Churchill's.

**Parliament Square,** the expanse of green between Westminster

Boadicea—the Celts' last hurrah

Parliament Square and Westminster Abbey

Abbey and Big Ben, is filled with statues of famous Brits such as **Winston Churchill,** the man who saved Britain from Hitler. According to tour guides, the statue has a current of electricity running through it to honor Churchill's wish that if a statue were made of him, his head wouldn't be soiled by pigeons. A few non-Brits are honored for their contributions to mankind, including **Nelson Mandela** (at opposite corner of the square) and **Abraham Lincoln** (far side of the square).

▶ *Consider touring Westminster Abbey (see the Westminster Abbey Tour chapter) or the Houses of Parliament (see page 122). Otherwise, patiently go back across the street, walk away from the Houses of Parliament and the Abbey, and continue (north) up the right side of Parliament Street, which becomes Whitehall.*

## ❹ Walking Along Whitehall

Today, Whitehall is choked with traffic, but imagine the effect this broad street must have had on out-of-towners a little more than a century ago. In your horse-drawn carriage, you'd clop along a tree-lined boulevard past well-dressed lords and ladies, dodging street urchins. You'd try to take it all in, your eyes dazzled by the bone-white walls of this manmade marble canyon.

Whitehall is now the most important street in Britain, lined with the ministries of finance, treasury, revenue and customs (the first on the left), and so on. You may see limos and camera crews as important dignitaries enter or exit. Notice the security measures. Iron grates seal off the concrete ditches alongside the buildings for protection against explosives. And concrete balustrades and black bollards protect key government departments and pedestrians alike.

▶ *Continue toward the tall, square stone monument in the middle of the boulevard.*

## ❺ Cenotaph

This monument honors those who died in World Wars I and II. The monumental devastation of these wars led to the drastic decline of the British Empire.

The actual cenotaph is the slab that sits atop the pillar—an empty tomb. You'll notice no religious symbols on this memorial. The dead honored here came from many creeds and all corners of Britain's empire. It looks lost in a sea of noisy cars, but on each Remembrance Sunday (closest to November 11), Whitehall is closed to traffic, the royal family fills the balcony overhead in the foreign ministry, and a memorial service is held around the cenotaph.

It was built to remember what Brits call "the Great War"—World War I. It's hard for an American to understand the war's long-term impact on Europe. On a single day (at the Battle of the Somme, 1916), the British suffered roughly as many casualties as the US did in the entire Vietnam War—nearly 60,000. It's said that if the roughly one million WWI dead from the British Empire were to march four abreast past the cenotaph, the sad parade would last for seven days.

▶ *Just past the cenotaph cross to the other (west) side of Whitehall, to the black iron security gate guarding the entrance to Downing Street.*

## ❻ #10 Downing Street and the Ministry of Defence

Britain's version of the White House is where the prime minister lives,

Whitehall—government and monuments     Cenotaph—grim reminder of two World Wars

at #10. It's the black-brick building 100 yards down the blocked-off street, on the right; there's a lantern and usually a security guard.

Like the White House's Rose Garden, the black door marked *10* is a highly symbolic point of power, popular for photo ops to mark big occasions. This is where suffragettes protested in the early 20th century, where Neville Chamberlain showed off his regrettable peace treaty with Hitler, and where David Cameron suffered his stunning Brexit defeat.

It looks modest, but #10's entryway does open up into fairly impressive digs—the prime minister's offices (downstairs), residence (upstairs), and two large formal dining rooms. The PM's staff has offices here. Many on the staff are permanent bureaucrats, staying on to serve as prime ministers come and go. The cabinet meets at #10 on Tuesday mornings. This is where foreign dignitaries come for official government dinners, where the prime minister receives honored schoolkids and victorious soccer teams, and where he gives monthly addresses to the nation. Next door, at #11, the chancellor of the exchequer (finance minister) lives with his family, and #12 houses the PM's press office.

This has been the traditional home of the prime minister since the position was created in the early 18th century. But even before that, the neighborhood (if not the building itself) was a center of power, where Edward the Confessor and Henry VIII had palaces. The facade is, frankly, quite cheap, having been built as part of a middle-class cul-de-sac of homes by American-born George Downing in the 1680s. When the first PM moved in, the humble interior was combined with a mansion in back. During a major upgrade in the 1950s, they discovered that the facade's black bricks were actually yellow—but had been

Heavy security for #10 Downing Street

Memorial to WWII women

stained by centuries of Industrial Age soot. To keep with tradition, they now paint the bricks black.

The guarded metal gates were installed in 1989 to protect against Irish terrorists. Even so, #10 was hit and partly damaged in 1991 by an Irish Republican Army mortar launched from a van. These days, there's typically not much to see unless a VIP happens to drive up. Then the bobbies snap to and check credentials, the gates open, the car is inspected for bombs, the traffic barrier midway down the street drops into its bat cave, the car drives in, and...the bobbies go back to mugging for the tourists.

The huge building across Whitehall from Downing Street is the **Ministry of Defence** (MOD), the "British Pentagon." This bleak place looks like a Ministry of Defence should. In front are statues of illustrious defenders of Britain, including **Field Marshal Bernard Law Montgomery** ("Monty"), who beat the Nazis in North Africa. (A **memorial** honoring the women who fought and died in World War II stands in the middle of the street.)

You may be enjoying the shade of London's **plane trees.** Their bark sheds and regenerates, which helps them survive in polluted London.

▸ *At the corner (same side as the Ministry of Defence), you'll find the...*

## ❼ Banqueting House

This two-story building is just about all that remains of what was once the biggest palace in Europe—Whitehall Palace, which once stretched from Trafalgar Square to Big Ben. Henry VIII started building it when he moved out of the Palace of Westminster (now the Parliament) and into the residence of the archbishop of York. Queen Elizabeth I and other monarchs added on as England's worldwide prestige grew.

Today, the exterior of Greek-style columns and pediments looks rather ho-hum, much like every other white marble building in London. But in 1620 it was a one-of-a-kind wonder—a big white temple rising above small half-timbered huts. Built by architect Inigo Jones, it sparked London's interest in the classical style. Within a century, London was awash in Georgian-style architecture, the English version of Neoclassical.

The Banqueting House was the site of one of the pivotal events of English history. On January 30, 1649, a man dressed in black stepped

Banqueting House—Neoclassical trendsetter    Horse Guard manning a symbolic checkpoint

out of one of the windows and onto a wooden platform. It was King Charles I. He gave a short speech to the crowd, then he knelt and laid his neck on a block as another man in black approached. It was the executioner—who cut off the king's head. Plop—the concept of divine monarchy in Britain was decapitated. Though the monarchy was restored a generation later, every ruler since then knows that the monarchy reigns by the grace of Parliament.

▶ *If you're interested in touring the impressive Banqueting House interior, see page 125. Otherwise, continue up Whitehall on the left (west) side, where you'll see (and smell) the building known as Horse Guards, guarded by traditionally dressed soldiers who are also called Horse Guards.*

## ❽ Horse Guards

For 200 years, soldiers in cavalry uniforms have guarded this arched entrance along Whitehall that leads to Buckingham Palace and one of its predecessors as royal residence, St. James's Palace.

Two different squads alternate, so depending on the day you visit, you'll see soldiers in either red coats with white plumes in their helmets (the Life Guards), or blue coats with red plumes (the Blues and Royals). Together, they constitute the Queen's personal bodyguard. Besides their ceremonial duties here in old-time uniforms, these elite troops have fought in Iraq and Afghanistan. Both Prince William and Prince Harry have served in the Blues and Royals.

The Horse Guards building was the headquarters of the British army from the time of the American Revolution until the Ministry of Defence was created in World War II. Through the arch is the broad expanse of the Horse Guards Parade, where troops parade to honor the monarch's birthday (Changing of the Guard is Mon-Sat at 11:00, Sun at 10:00, dismounting ceremony daily at 16:00, get the latest at www. changing-guard.com). The Household Cavalry Museum (through the arch and to the right) offers a glimpse at the stables and a collection of uniforms and weapons.

▶ *Continue up Whitehall, passing the Old Admiralty (#26, on left), headquarters of the British navy that once ruled the waves. Across the street, behind the old Clarence Pub, stood the original Scotland Yard, headquarters of London's crack police force in the days of Sherlock Holmes. Finally, Whitehall opens up into the grand, noisy, traffic-filled Trafalgar Square.*

## ❾ Trafalgar Square

London's central meeting point bustles around the world's biggest Corinthian column, where **Admiral Horatio Nelson** stands 170 feet off the ground, looking over London in the direction of one of the greatest naval battles in history. Nelson saved England at a time as dark as World War II. In 1805, Napoleon was poised on the other side of the Channel, threatening to invade. Meanwhile, more than 900 miles away, the one-armed, one-eyed, and one-minded Lord Nelson attacked the French fleet off the coast of Spain at Trafalgar. The French were routed, Britannia ruled the waves, and the once-invincible French army was slowly worn down, then defeated at Waterloo. Nelson, while victorious, was shot by a sniper in the battle. He epitomized British pluck when he died, gasping, "Thank God, I have done my duty."

At the base of Nelson's column are bronze reliefs cast from melted-down enemy cannons, and four huggable lions dying to have their photo taken with you. The nearby fountains, lit by colored lights, can shoot water 80 feet in the air. There are numerous (somewhat boring) statues that dot the square. But focus on the pedestal on the northwest corner (the "fourth plinth"), which is periodically topped with contemporary art.

Make your way to the top of the square and take in your surroundings. Trafalgar Square is the center of modern London, connecting Westminster, The City, and the West End. Spin clockwise 360 degrees and survey the city:

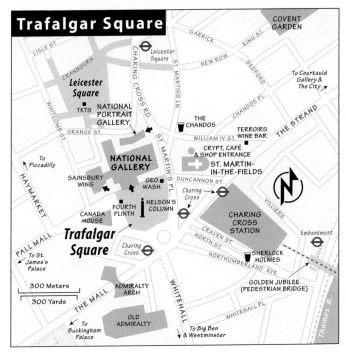

To the south (down Whitehall) is the center of government, Westminster. Looking southwest, through the Admiralty Arch and down the broad boulevard called The Mall, you can see Buckingham Palace in the distance. (Down Pall Mall is St. James's Palace and Clarence House, where Prince Charles lives when in London.) A few blocks northwest of Trafalgar Square is Piccadilly Circus. Directly north (a block behind the National Gallery) sits Leicester Square, the jumping-off point for Soho, Covent Garden, and the West End theater district.

The boulevard called the Strand takes you past Charing Cross Station, then eastward to The City, the original walled town of London and today's financial center. In medieval times, when people from The City met with the Westminster government, it was here. And finally,

Trafalgar Square—full of fountains, people, and statues—is the thriving center of the city.

Northumberland Street leads southeast to the Golden Jubilee pedestrian bridge over the Thames. Along the way, you'll pass the Sherlock Holmes Pub (just off Northumberland Street, on Craven Passage), housed in Sir Arthur Conan Doyle's favorite watering hole, with an upstairs replica of 221b Baker Street.

Soak it in. You're smack-dab in the center of London, a thriving city atop two millennia of history.

# Westminster Abbey Tour

Westminster Abbey is the most famous English church in Christendom, where the nation's royalty has been wedded, crowned, and buried since the 11th century. The histories of Westminster Abbey and England are almost the same. A thousand years of English history (and 3,000 tombs) lie within its stained-glass splendor and under its stone slabs.

On this hour-plus walk, we'll stroll through the elaborate Gothic architecture of the church and see some of England's dearly departed, including the tombs of 29 kings and queens. We'll see memorials to England's greatest politicians, scientists, writers, and warriors. And—in the heart of the church—we'll visit the spot where, one fine day, Prince Charles (or William or little George) will be crowned the next King of England.

# ORIENTATION

**Cost:** £23, £5 more for timed-entry ticket to Queen's Diamond Jubilee Galleries, family ticket available, cheaper online, includes fine audioguide.

**Hours:** Abbey—Mon-Fri 9:30-16:30, Wed until 19:00 (main church only), Sat 9:00-16:00 (Sept-April until 14:00); Queen's Galleries—Mon-Fri 10:00-16:00, Sat 9:30-15:30; cloister—Mon-Sat 8:00-18:00; closed Sun to sightseers but open for services; last entry one hour before closing. Special events can curtail hours; check website before you go.

**Information:** Tel. 020/7222-5152, www.westminster-abbey.org.

**Timed-Entry Tickets:** Avoid long ticket-buying lines (especially in summer) by buying a timed-entry ticket on the Abbey's website. Book the Queen's Galleries entry about an hour after your Abbey visit time.

**When to Go:** It's most crowded midmorning and all day Sat and Mon. Weekdays after 14:30 are less congested; come late and stay for the 17:00 evensong.

**Dress Code:** None, even for services.

**Getting There:** Near Big Ben and the Houses of Parliament (Tube: Westminster or St. James's Park).

**Church Services and Music:** Evensong Mon-Fri 17:00, Sat-Sun 15:00 (May-Aug Sat at 17:00). Check website for church service schedule. Sun services generally come with more music. Services are free to anyone, though visitors who haven't paid church admission aren't allowed to linger afterward. Free organ recitals many Sundays at 17:45.

**Tours:** The included audioguide is excellent. Entertaining 1.5-hour £5 guided tours leave up to six times a day in summer.

**Eating:** The cloister has a **$$ café.** Other options nearby: **$ Wesley's Café,** in the basement of Methodist Central Hall across the street, serves cheap breakfast and lunch (Mon-Fri 8:00-16:00, Sat-Sun from 9:00); **$$ The Westminster Arms,** just past the Methodist Central Hall on Storey's Gate, serves pub grub (daily 12:00-20:00).

**Starring:** Edwards, Elizabeths, Henrys, Annes, Marys, and poets.

# THE TOUR BEGINS

You'll have no choice but to follow the steady flow of tourists through the church, along the route laid out for the audioguide. It's all one-way, and most days the crowds are a real crush. Here are the Abbey's top stops.

▶ *Walk straight in, entering the north transept. Pick up the map/flier and audioguide. Follow the crowd flow to the right, passing through a number of...*

## ❶ Memorials (the First of Many)

Westminster Abbey has become a place where the nation comes to remember its own. You'll pass by statues on tombs, stained glass on walls, and plaques in the floor, all honoring illustrious Brits, both famous and not so famous. Keep an eye out for **Scientists' Corner,** a cluster of memorials. There's one for Charles Darwin (plaque on the floor), star-watcher William Herschel (also on floor), Isaac Newton (statue on corner of the choir), and pioneer in electricity Michael Faraday (on the floor beneath Newton). In 2018, physicist Stephen Hawking was laid to rest near Newton. His plaque on the floor depicts a black hole, along with his breakthrough equation that calculates the temperature ($T$) of a black hole's subtle radiation.

Continuing on, you'll pass by stained-glass portraits of illustrious kings and bishops and names of significant "civil engineers." In display cases are books of remembrance with names of soldiers who gave their lives. At the end of the aisle is Prime Minister's Corner, with the graves of Clement Attlee, Harold MacMillan, and Harold Wilson.

▶ *Now enter the spacious nave and take it all in.*

## ❷ Nave

Look down the long and narrow center aisle of the church. Lined with the praying hands of the Gothic arches, glowing with light from the stained glass, this is more than a museum. With saints in stained glass, heroes in carved stone, and the bodies of England's greatest citizens under the floor stones, Westminster Abbey is the religious heart of England.

The Abbey was built in 1065. Its name, Westminster, means Church in the West (west of St. Paul's Cathedral). The king who built the Abbey was Edward the Confessor. Find him in the stained glass

Memorials to great Britons in the nave

Crisscross vaults in this medieval church

windows on the left side of the nave as you face the altar. He's in the third bay from the end (marked *S: Edwardus rex...*), dressed in white and blue, with his crown, scepter, and ring.

The Abbey's 10-story nave is the tallest in England. The sleek chandeliers, 10 feet tall, look small in comparison (16 were given to the Abbey by the Guinness family).

On the floor near the west entrance of the Abbey is the flower-lined **Grave of the Unknown Warrior,** one ordinary WWI soldier buried in soil from France with lettering made from melted-down weapons. Contemplate the 800,000 men from the British Empire who gave their lives. Their memory is so revered that, when Kate Middleton walked up the aisle on her wedding day, by tradition she had to step around the tomb. Hanging on a column next to the tomb is the US Medal of Honor, presented by General John J. Pershing in 1921 to honor England's WWI dead. Closer to the door is a memorial to a hero of World War II, Winston Churchill.

▶ *Now walk straight up the nave toward the altar. This is the same route every future monarch walks on the way to being crowned. Midway up the nave, you pass through the colorful screen of an enclosure known as the...*

### ❸ Choir

These elaborately carved wood and gilded seats are where monks once chanted their services in the "quire"—as it's known in British church-speak. Today, it's where the Abbey's boys choir sings the evensong. You're approaching the center of this cross-shaped church. Up ahead, the "high" (main) altar—which usually has a cross and candlesticks atop it—sits on the platform up the five stairs. It's on this platform that the monarch is crowned.

# Westminster Abbey Tour

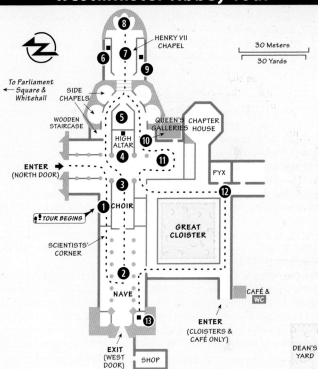

To Parliament
Square &
Whitehall

HENRY VII
CHAPEL

30 Meters
30 Yards

SIDE
CHAPELS

WOODEN
STAIRCASE

HIGH
ALTAR

QUEEN'S
GALLERIES

CHAPTER
HOUSE

PYX

ENTER
(NORTH DOOR)

TOUR BEGINS

CHOIR

SCIENTISTS'
CORNER

GREAT
CLOISTER

NAVE

CAFÉ &
WC

ENTER
(CLOISTERS &
CAFÉ ONLY)

DEAN'S
YARD

EXIT
(WEST
DOOR)

SHOP

❶ Memorials
❷ Nave
❸ Choir
❹ Coronation Spot
❺ Shrine of Edward the Confessor
❻ Tomb of Elizabeth I & Mary I
❼ Chapel of King Henry VII

❽ Royal Air Force Chapel
❾ Tomb of Mary, Queen of Scots
❿ Queen's Diamond
   Jubilee Galleries
⓫ Poets' Corner
⓬ Great Cloister
⓭ Coronation Chair

## ❹ Coronation Spot

The area immediately before the high altar is where every English coronation since 1066 has taken place. Imagine the day when Prince William becomes king.

The nobles in robes and powdered wigs look on from the carved wooden stalls of the choir. The Archbishop of Canterbury stands at the high altar. The coronation chair (which we'll see later) is placed before the altar on the round, brown pavement stone representing the earth. Surrounding the whole area are temporary bleachers for 8,000 VIPs, going halfway up the rose windows of each transept, creating a "theater."

Long silver trumpets hung with banners sound a fanfare as the monarch-to-be enters the church. The congregation sings, "I will go into the house of the Lord," as William parades slowly down the nave and up the steps to the altar. After a church service, he sits in the chair, facing the altar, where the crown jewels are placed. William is anointed with holy oil, then receives a ceremonial sword, ring, and cup. The royal scepter is placed in his hands, and—*dut dutta dah*—the archbishop lowers the Crown of St. Edward the Confessor onto his royal head. Finally, King William V stands up, descends the steps, and is presented to the people. As cannons roar throughout the city, the people cry, "God save the king!"

The Abbey is also the place for royal funerals (Princess Diana's in 1997, the Queen's mother in 2002) and for weddings (Queen Elizabeth II and Prince Philip in 1947). In 2011, Prince William and Kate Middleton strolled up the nave, passed through the choir, climbed the five steps to the high altar, and became husband and wife—and the future king and queen of the United Kingdom and its Commonwealth.

▶ *Now veer left and detour as you wish into the side chapels—the Chapel of St. Michael and Chapel of St. John the Baptist. In this land of dead kings and queens, you'll see effigies of the dead lying atop their tombs of polished stone.*

*After exploring the chapels, pause at the wooden staircase on your right.*

## ❺ Shrine of Edward the Confessor

The holiest part of the church is the raised area behind the altar (where the wooden staircase leads—sorry, no tourist access except with verger tour). Step back and peek over the dark coffin of Edward I

The wooden seats of the choir—nestled in the spacious nave—are for clergy and singers.

to see the tippy-top of the green-and-gold wedding-cake tomb of King Edward the Confessor—the man who built Westminster Abbey. It was finished just in time to bury Edward and to crown his foreign successor, William the Conqueror, in 1066.

▶ *At the top of the stone staircase, veer left into the private burial chapel of Queen Elizabeth I.*

## ❻ Tomb of Queens Elizabeth I and Mary I

Although only one effigy is on the tomb (Elizabeth's), there are actually two queens buried beneath it, both daughters of Henry VIII (by different mothers). Bloody Mary—meek, pious, sickly, and Catholic—enforced Catholicism during her short reign (1553-1558) by burning "heretics" at the stake.

Elizabeth—strong, clever, and Protestant—steered England on an Anglican course. She holds a royal orb symbolizing that she's queen of the whole globe. When 26-year-old Elizabeth was crowned in the Abbey, her right to rule was questioned because she was considered the bastard seed of Henry VIII's unsanctioned marriage to Anne Boleyn. But Elizabeth's long reign (1559-1603) was one of the greatest in English history, a time when England ruled the seas and Shakespeare explored human emotions. When she died, thousands turned out for her funeral in the Abbey. Elizabeth's face on the tomb, modeled after her death mask, is considered a very accurate take on this hook-nosed, imperious "Virgin Queen" (she never married).

The two half-sisters disliked each other in life—Mary even had Elizabeth locked up in the Tower of London for a short time. Now they lie side by side for eternity. The Latin inscription ends, "Here we lie, two sisters in hope of one resurrection."

▶ *Continue into the ornate, flag-draped room behind the main altar.*

## ❼ Chapel of King Henry VII (the Lady Chapel)

The light from the stained-glass windows; the colorful banners overhead; and the elaborate tracery in stone, wood, and glass give this room the festive air of a medieval tournament. The prestigious Knights of the Bath meet here, under the magnificent ceiling studded with gold pendants. The ceiling—of carved stone, not plaster (1519)—is a textbook example of English Perpendicular Gothic and fan vaulting. The ceiling was sculpted on the floor in pieces, then jigsaw-puzzled into place.

The knights sit in the wooden stalls with their coats of arms on the back, churches on their heads, their banner flying above, and the graves of kings beneath their feet. When the Queen worships here, she sits in the corner chair—the one topped with the lion crown.

Behind the small altar is an iron cage housing tombs of Henry VII of Lancaster and his wife, Elizabeth of York, whose marriage finally settled the Wars of the Roses between the two clans. Henry VII, the first Tudor king, was the father of Henry VIII and the grandfather of Elizabeth I. This exuberant chapel heralds a new optimistic postwar era as England prepares to step onto the world stage.

▶ *At the far end of the chapel is a modern set of stained-glass windows.*

## ❽ Royal Air Force Chapel

Saints in robes and halos mingle with pilots in parachutes and bomber jackets. This tribute to WWII flyers is for those who earned their angel wings in the Battle of Britain (July-Oct 1940). When Hitler's air force threatened to snuff Britain out without a fight, British pilots stepped up. These were the pilots about whom Churchill said, "Never...was so much owed by so many to so few."

The Abbey survived the Battle and the Blitz, but this window did not, so it was replaced with this modern memorial. The book of remembrances lists the 1,497 airmen (including one American) who died in the Battle of Britain.

▶ *Exit the Chapel of Henry VII. Turn left into a side chapel with the tomb (the central one of three in the chapel).*

## ❾ Tomb of Mary, Queen of Scots

Historians get dewy-eyed over the fate of Mary, Queen of Scots

Elizabeth I, buried alongside her sister and rival

Chapel of King Henry VII—exuberant Gothic

(1542-1587). The beautiful ruler of Scotland (then an independent country) was executed for treason by her cousin, Queen Elizabeth I. When Elizabeth died childless, Mary's son—James VI, King of Scots—also became King James I of England and Ireland. James honored his mum with the Abbey's most sumptuous tomb.

▶ *Exit Mary's chapel. Ahead of you, again, is the tomb of the church's founder, Edward the Confessor. Continue on, until you emerge in the south transept. Look for the doorway that leads to a stairway and elevator to the...*

## ⑩ Queen's Diamond Jubilee Galleries

This balcony—with stunning views over the nave—houses a small museum of interesting objects related to the Abbey's construction, the monarchs who worshipped here, royal coronations, and more from its 1,000-year history. This space—known as the triforium—had been closed off for 700 years and reopened in 2018.

Among the highlights you may see are small-scale versions of the statues of the 20th-century Christian martyrs that stand above the Abbey's main (west) door, including Martin Luther King, Jr. Some of the Abbey's oldest stones are the 900-year-old column capitals on display, curiously carved with faces and scenes. You'll also see funeral effigies of monarchs, from the first crude wooden statue (of Edward III) to psychologically probing portraits (like Henry VII and his wife Elizabeth of York) to elaborately dressed, Madame Tussaud-quality wax figures.

▶ *Return to the main floor. You're in...*

## ⑪ Poets' Corner

England's greatest artistic contributions are in the written word. Here the masters of arguably the world's most complex and expressive language are remembered. (Many writers are honored with plaques and monuments; relatively few are actually buried here.)

▶ *Start with Chaucer, buried in the wall under the blue windows, marked with a white plaque reading* Qui Fuit Anglorum...

**Geoffrey Chaucer** (c. 1343-1400) is often considered the father of English literature. Chaucer's *Canterbury Tales* told of earthy people speaking everyday English, not French or Latin. He was the first great writer buried in the Abbey (thanks to his job as a Westminster clerk). Later, it became a tradition to bury other writers here, and Poets'

Shakespeare's memorial in Poets' Corner: "I would give all my fame for a pot of ale..."

Corner was built around his tomb. The blue windows have blank panels awaiting the names of future poets.

▶ *The plaques on the floor before Chaucer are gravestones and memorials to other literary greats.*

**Lord Byron,** the great lover of women and adventure: "Though the night was made for loving, / And the day returns too soon, / Yet we'll go no more a-roving / By the light of the moon."

**Dylan Thomas,** alcoholic master of modernism, with a Romantic's heart: "Oh as I was young and easy in the mercy of his means, / Time held me green and dying / Though I sang in my chains like the sea."

**Alfred, Lord Tennyson,** conscience of the Victorian era: "'Tis better to have loved and lost / Than never to have loved at all."

**Robert Browning:** "Oh, to be in England / Now that April's there."

▶ *Farther out in the south transept, you'll find a statue of...*

**William Shakespeare:** Although he's not buried here, a fine statue honors him: "Life's but a walking shadow, a poor player that struts and frets his hour upon the stage and then is heard no more."

**George Frideric Handel:** High on the wall opposite Shakespeare is the German immigrant famous for composing the *Messiah* oratorio:

"Hallelujah, hallelujah, hallelujah." His actual tomb is on the floor, next to...

**Charles Dickens,** whose serialized novels brought literature to the masses: "It was the best of times, it was the worst of times."

Finally, near the center of the transept, find the small, white floor plaque of **Thomas Parr** (marked *THO: PARR*). Check the dates of his life (1483-1635) and do the math. In his (reputed) 152 years, he served 10 sovereigns and was a contemporary of Columbus, Henry VIII, Elizabeth I, Shakespeare, and Galileo.

▶ *Exit the church (temporarily) at the south door, which leads to the...*

## ⑫ Great Cloister

The buildings that adjoin the church housed the monks. (The church is known as the "abbey" because it was the headquarters of the Benedictine Order until Henry VIII kicked them out in 1540.) Cloistered courtyards like this gave them a place to stroll in peace while meditating on God's creations.

The **Chapter House** is where the monks had daily meetings. It features fine architecture and stained glass, some faded but well-described medieval paintings and floor tiles, and—in the corridor—Britain's oldest door. A few steps farther down the hall is the **Pyx Chamber,** which once safeguarded the coins used to set the silver standard of the realm.

As you continue circling the cloister, meditate on the **flying buttresses,** the stone bridges that push in on the church walls and allow Gothic architects to build so high.

▶ *Go back into the church for the last stop.*

## ⑬ Coronation Chair

A gold-painted oak chair waits here under a regal canopy for the next coronation. For every English coronation since 1308 (except two), it's been moved to its spot before the high altar to receive the royal buttocks. The chair's legs rest on lions, England's symbol. The space below the chair originally held a big sandstone rock from Scotland called the Stone of Scone (pronounced "skoon"), symbolizing Scotland's unity with England's monarch. But in the 1990s, Britain gave Scotland more sovereignty, its own Parliament, and the Stone,

The cloister—covered walkways for monks        Coronation chair with slot for Stone of Scone

which Scotland has agreed to loan to Britain for future coronations (the rest of the time, it's on display in Edinburgh Castle).

Next to the chapel with the chair hangs a 600-year-old portrait of King Richard II. The boy king holds the royal orb and scepter, dons the crown, and takes his seat upon this very chair.

Finally, take one last look down the nave. Listen to and ponder this place, filled with the remains of the people who made Britain a world power—saints, royalty, poets, musicians, scientists, soldiers, politicians. Now step back outside into a city filled with the modern-day poets, saints, and heroes who continue to make Britain great.

# National Gallery Tour

The National Gallery lets you tour Europe's art without ever crossing the Channel. Britain's best collection of paintings features all the biggies: Leonardo da Vinci, Rembrandt, Monet, Van Gogh, and more. The "National Gal" is always a welcome interlude from the bustle of London sightseeing.

In this 90-minute tour we'll travel chronologically through art history: from medieval holiness to Renaissance realism, from Dutch detail to Baroque bombast, from British restraint to the colorful French Impressionism that leads to the modern world. We'll cruise like an eagle with wide eyes for the big picture, seeing how each style progresses into the next.

# ORIENTATION

**Cost:** Free, £5 suggested donation; special exhibits extra.

**Hours:** Daily 10:00-18:00, Fri until 21:00, last entry to special exhibits 45 minutes before closing.

**Information:** Tel. 020/7747-2885, www.nationalgallery.org.uk.

**Getting There:** It's as central as can be, overlooking Trafalgar Square (Tube: Charing Cross or Leicester Square). Handy buses #9, #11, #15, and #24 (among others) pass by.

**Tours:** Free one-hour overview tours leave from the Sainsbury Wing info desk Mon-Fri at 14:00. The excellent £5 audioguides offer an array of tours, including one that lets you dial up info on any painting.

**Services:** Cloakrooms are at each entrance (£2 for bags). You can take a small bag into the museum.

**Cuisine Art:** There are three eateries in the National Gallery. The **$$$ National Dining Rooms,** on the first floor of the Sainsbury Wing, has a classy table-service menu. The **$$$ National Café,** near the Getty Entrance, has a table-service restaurant and a cheaper adjoining café. The **$ Espresso Bar,** near the Portico and Getty entrances, has sandwiches and pastries. Outside the Gallery, several options are on or near Trafalgar Square (see page 184).

# THE TOUR BEGINS

The Gallery has three entrances facing Trafalgar Square. Our tour starts from the Sainsbury Entrance, in the annex to the left of the classic building. The paintings are all on one floor. To see the art in chronological order requires a bit of map-reading and navigating, but it's worth it.

▶ *Pick up the handy map (£2) and climb the stairs. At the top, turn left, then left again, entering Room 51.*

## Medieval (1200s-Early 1400s)

In Room 51 (and nearby rooms), shiny gold paintings of saints, angels, Madonnas, and crucifixions float in an ethereal gold never-never land.

One thing is very clear: Medieval heaven was different from medieval earth. The holy wore gold plates on their heads. Faces were serene and generic. People posed stiffly, facing either directly out or to the side, never in between. Saints are recognized by the symbols they carry (a key, a sword, a book), rather than by their human features. Art in the Middle Ages was religious, dominated by the Church. The illiterate faithful could meditate on an altarpiece and visualize heaven. It's as though they couldn't imagine saints and angels inhabiting the dreary world of rocks, trees, and sky they lived in.

▶ *One of the finest medieval altarpieces is tucked in the small alcove in Room 51.*

### ❶ Anonymous, *The Wilton Diptych*, c. 1395-1399

Three kings (left panel) come to adore Mary and her rosy-cheeked baby (right panel), surrounded by flame-like angels. The kings have expressive faces, and the back side shows a deer in the grass. Still, the anonymous artist is struggling with reality. The figures are flat, scrawny, and sinless. Mary's exquisite fingers hold an anatomically impossible little foot. John the Baptist (among the kings) is holding a "lamb of God" that looks more like a Chihuahua. Nice try.

▶ *Head into adjoining Room 60, and turn left into Room 59, entering the...*

## Early Italian Renaissance (1400s)

The Renaissance—or "rebirth" of the culture of ancient Greece and Rome—was a cultural boom that changed people's thinking about every aspect of life. In politics, it meant democracy. In religion, it meant a move away from Church dominance and toward the assertion of man (humanism) and a more personal faith. Science and secular learning were revived after centuries of superstition and ignorance. In architecture, it was a return to the balanced columns and domes of Greece and Rome. In painting, the Renaissance meant realism. Artists rediscovered the beauty of nature and the human body. With pictures of beautiful people in harmonious 3-D surroundings, they expressed the optimism and confidence of this new age.

### ❷ Uccello, *Battle of San Romano*, c. 1438-1440

This colorful battle scene shows Florence's victory over Siena—and

NATIONAL GALLERY TOUR

## MEDIEVAL
**1** ANONYMOUS – The Wilton Diptych

## EARLY ITALIAN RENAISSANCE
**2** UCCELLO – Battle of San Romano
**3** BOTTICELLI – Venus and Mars
**4** CRIVELLI – The Annunciation, with Saint Emidius
**5** LEONARDO – The Virgin of the Rocks
**6** LEONARDO – Virgin and Child with St. Anne and St. John the Baptist
**7** VAN EYCK – The Arnolfini Portrait

## HIGH RENAISSANCE
**8** MICHELANGELO – The Entombment
**9** RAPHAEL – Pope Julius II

## MANNERISM
**10** BRONZINO – An Allegory with Venus and Cupid
**11** TINTORETTO – The Origin of the Milky Way

## NORTHERN PROTESTANT ART
**12** VERMEER – A Young Woman Standing at a Virginal

## BAROQUE
**13** RUBENS – The Judgment of Paris
**14** REMBRANDT – Self-Portrait at the Age of 63
**15** REMBRANDT – Belshazzar's Feast
**16** VELÁZQUEZ – The Rokeby Venus
**17** VAN DYCK – Equestrian Portrait of Charles I
**18** CARAVAGGIO –The Supper at Emmaus

## FRENCH ROCOCO
**19** BOUCHER – Pan and Syrinx

To Leicester Square ⊖↑
(5-min. walk)

## SAINSBURY WING

ENTRANCE ON LEVEL 0

SELF-GUIDED TOUR
STARTS ON LEVEL 2

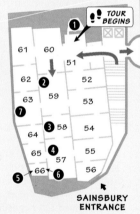

👣 TOUR BEGINS

61 60
51
62 59 52
63 53
7
64 3 58 54
65 4 57 55
5 66 6 56

SAINSBURY ENTRANCE

## BRITISH ROMANTIC ART
**20** CONSTABLE – The Hay Wain
**21** TURNER – The Fighting Téméraire

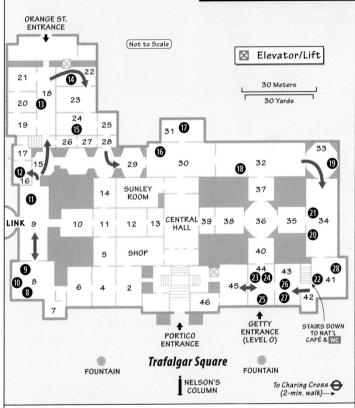

# National Gallery

ORANGE ST. ENTRANCE

Not to Scale

⊠ Elevator/Lift

30 Meters

30 Yards

LINK

SUNLEY ROOM

CENTRAL HALL

SHOP

PORTICO ENTRANCE

GETTY ENTRANCE (LEVEL 0)

STAIRS DOWN TO NAT'L CAFÉ & WC

*Trafalgar Square*

FOUNTAIN

NELSON'S COLUMN

FOUNTAIN

To Charing Cross (2-min. walk)→

## IMPRESSIONISM & BEYOND

**22** MONET – The Water-Lily Pond

**23** MONET – Gare St. Lazare

**24** MANET – Corner of a Café-Concert

**25** RENOIR – The Skiff

**26** SEURAT – Bathers at Asnières

**27** VAN GOGH – Sunflowers

**28** CÉZANNE – Bathers

*The Wilton Diptych*—scrawny medieval figures     Uccello creates a 3-D grid.

the battle for literal realism on the canvas. It's an early Renaissance attempt at a realistic, nonreligious, three-dimensional scene.

Uccello challenges the illusion of distance with a background of farmyards, receding hedges, and tiny soldiers. He actually constructs a grid of fallen lances in the foreground, then places the horses and warriors within it. Still, Uccello hasn't quite worked out the bugs—the figures in the distance are far too big, and the fallen soldier on the left isn't much larger than the fallen shield on the right.

▸ *Continue into Room 58, where the classical age is being "reborn."*

### ❸ Botticelli, *Venus and Mars*, c. 1485

Mars takes a break from war, succumbing to the delights of love (Venus), while impish satyrs play innocently with the discarded tools of death. In the early spring of the Renaissance, there was an optimistic mood in the air—the feeling that enlightened Man could solve all problems. Venus has sapped man's medieval stiffness; the Renaissance has arrived.

▸ *Continue into Room 57.*

### ❹ Crivelli, *The Annunciation, with Saint Emidius*, 1486

Mary, in green, is visited by the dove of the Holy Spirit, who beams down from the distant heavens in a shaft of light. It's a brilliant collection of realistic details: the hanging rug, the peacock, the architectural minutiae that lead you way, way back, then *bam!*—you have a giant pickle in your face.

It combines meticulous detail with Italian spaciousness. The floor tiles and building bricks recede into the distance. We're sucked

Botticelli revives ancient Greek symbols.

Crivelli's illusion requires no 3-D glasses.

right in, accelerating through the alleyway, under the arch, and off into space. The Holy Spirit spans the entire distance, connecting heavenly background with earthly foreground. Crivelli creates an Escheresque labyrinth of rooms and walkways that we want to walk through, around, and into—or is that just a male thing?

Renaissance Italians were interested in—even obsessed with—portraying 3-D space. Perhaps they focused their spiritual passion away from heaven and toward the physical world. With such restless energy, they needed lots of elbow room. Space, the final frontier.

▶ *Enter adjoining Room 65, then left into Room 66, with works by the genius who put all these budding Renaissance techniques together.*

### ❺ Leonardo, *The Virgin of the Rocks*, c. 1491-1508

Mary, the mother of Jesus, plays with her son and Johnny the Baptist (with cross, at left) while an androgynous angel looks on. Leonardo brings this holy scene right down to earth by setting it among rocks, stalactites, water, and flowering plants. But looking closer, we see that Leonardo has deliberately posed his people into a pyramid shape, with Mary's head at the peak, creating an oasis of maternal stability and serenity amid the hard rock of the earth. Leonardo, who was born illegitimate, may have sought in his art the young mother he never knew. Freud thought so.

▶ *Nearby is a drawing of a similar-looking scene.*

### ❻ Leonardo, *Virgin and Child with St. Anne and St. John the Baptist*, c. 1499-1500

This chalk cartoon (a full-size preparatory drawing for a painting)

Leonardo's *Virgin*—a maternal pyramid

Leonardo's sketch—all eyes lead to Jesus.

shows two children at play—oblivious to the violent deaths they'll both suffer—beneath their mothers' Mona Lisa smiles.

But follow the eyes: Shadowy-eyed Anne turns toward Mary, who looks tenderly down to Jesus, who blesses John, who gazes back dreamily. As your eyes follow theirs, you're led back to the literal and psychological center of the composition—Jesus—the Alpha and Omega. This sketch—pieced together from two separate papers (see the line down the middle)—gives us an inside peek at Leonardo's genius.

▶ *In Room 63, find the Netherlandish masterpiece...*

## ❼ Van Eyck, *The Arnolfini Portrait*, 1434

Called by some "The Shotgun Wedding," this painting was once thought to depict a wedding ceremony forced by the lady's swelling belly. Today it's understood as a portrait of a solemn, well-dressed, well-heeled couple, the Arnolfinis of Bruges, Belgium. It is a masterpiece of down-to-earth details.

Feel the texture of the fabrics, count the terrier's hairs, trace the shadows generated by the window. Each object is shown in close-up focus, so the beads on the back wall are as crystal clear as the bracelets on the woman. To top it off, the round mirror on the far wall reflects the whole scene backward in miniature, showing the loving couple and a pair of mysterious visitors. Is one of them Van Eyck himself at his easel? Or has the artist painted you, the home viewer, into the scene?

By the way, the woman likely is not pregnant. The fashion of the day was to gather up the folds of one's extremely full-skirted dress. At least, that's what they told her parents.

*The Arnolfini Portrait*—Flemish artists meticulously captured everyday events. Details, details.

▶ *Return to Room 51, cross to the main building (West Wing) and enter Room 9. Turn right and exit into Room 8 to enter the...*

## High Renaissance (1490s-early 1500s)

The Renaissance was born in Florence, but it flowered in Venice and Rome, before spreading north to the rest of Europe. The "Big Three" of the High Renaissance—Leonardo, Michelangelo, and Raphael—were all Florence-trained. Like Renaissance architects (which they also were), they carefully composed their figures on canvas, "building" them into geometrical patterns that reflected the balance and order they saw in nature.

In Venice—a city grown wealthy by trading with the luxurious and exotic East—artists forged a happy-go-lucky art style that shows a taste for the finer things in life. Madonnas and saints were replaced by smooth-skinned, sexy, golden centerfolds. Venetian artists revived the classical world in all its pagan glory, creating beautiful scenes of sensuous Nature.

### ❽ Michelangelo, *The Entombment*, c. 1500-1501

Michelangelo, the greatest sculptor ever, proves it here in this "painted sculpture" of the crucified Jesus being carried to the tomb. Like a chiseled Greek god, this musclehead in red ripples beneath his clothes. Christ's naked body, shocking to the medieval Church, was completely acceptable in the Renaissance world, where classical nudes were admired as an expression of the divine. Regardless of the lack of detail, Michelangelo lets the bodies do the talking.

Renaissance balance and symmetry reign. Christ is the center of the composition, flanked by two people leaning equally who support his body with strips of cloth. They, in turn, are flanked by two others.

The painting is not damaged, but it is unfinished. Michelangelo, 25 years old at the time, moved on to other projects before he got around to adding crucial details, even leaving a blank space in the lower right where Mary would have been.

### ❾ Raphael, *Pope Julius II*, 1511

The new worldliness of the Renaissance even reached the Church. Pope Julius II, who was more a swaggering conquistador than a pious pope, set out to rebuild Rome in Renaissance style, hiring Michelangelo to paint the ceiling of the Vatican's Sistine Chapel.

Michelangelo's bodybuilder saints

Raphael—psychological realism

Raphael gives a behind-the-scenes look at this complex leader. On the one hand, the pope is an imposing pyramid of power, with a velvet shawl, silk shirt, and fancy rings boasting of wealth and success. But at the same time, he's a bent and broken man, his throne backed into a corner, with an expression that seems to say, "Is this all there is?"

▶ *And now for something completely different, still in Room 8.*

## Mannerism (1520s–1600)

Mannerism, developed in reaction to the High Renaissance, subverts the balanced, harmonious ideal of the previous era with exaggerated proportions, asymmetrical compositions, and decorative color.

### ⓾ Bronzino, *An Allegory with Venus and Cupid,* c. 1545

The right foot of the figure of boy Cupid (standing on the left) was used in the old TV comedy show *Monty Python's Flying Circus.* As the show opened and circus music played, Cupid's giant foot would come down from above to squash the scene with a flatulent *ffft!*

▶ *Return to Room 9. As you pass through, you may catch sight of a naked woman and man spinning in midair.*

### ⓫ Tintoretto, *The Origin of the Milky Way,* c. 1575

The promiscuous god Jupiter places his illegitimate son, baby Hercules, at his wife's breast. Juno says, "Wait a minute. That's not my baby!" Her milk spurts upward, becoming the Milky Way.

Tintoretto places us right up in the clouds among the gods, who swirl around at every angle. Jupiter appears to be flying almost right at

Bronzino—detail of Venus and Cupid feeling frisky    Tintoretto—"That's not my baby!"

us. An X composition unites it all—Juno slants one way while Jupiter tilts the other.

▶ *Exit Room 9 at the far end and immediately turn left into small Room 16.*

## Northern Protestant Art (1600s)

We switch from CinemaScope to a tiny TV—smaller canvases, subdued colors, everyday scenes, and not even a bare shoulder.

Money shapes art. The northern country's art buyers were middle-class, hardworking, Protestant merchants. They wanted simple, cheap, no-nonsense pictures to decorate their homes and offices. Greek gods and Virgin Marys were out, hometown folks and hometown places were in—portraits, landscapes, still lifes, and slice-of-life scenes. Painted with great attention to detail, this is art meant not to wow or preach at you, but to be enjoyed and lingered over. Sightsee.

## ⑫ Vermeer, *A Young Woman Standing at a Virginal*, c. 1670

Inside a simple but wealthy Dutch home, a prim virgin plays an early piano called a "virginal." We've surprised her, and she pauses to look up at us.

By framing off such a small world to look at—from the blue chair in the foreground to the wall in back—Vermeer forces us to appreciate the tiniest details, the beauty of everyday things. We can meditate on the tiles lining the floor, the subtle shades of the white wall, and the pale, diffused light that seeps in from the window. The painting of a nude cupid on the back wall only strengthens this virgin's purity.

▶ *Exit into the octagonal rotunda, then into Room 18.*

## Baroque (1600s)

This room holds big, colorful, emotional works by Peter Paul Rubens

Vermeer explores the beauty of everyday things.

and others from Catholic Flanders (Belgium). While artists in Protestant and democratic Europe painted simple scenes, those in Catholic and aristocratic countries turned to the style called Baroque. Baroque art took what was flashy in Venetian art and made it flashier, what was gaudy and made it gaudier, what was dramatic and made it shocking.

### ⑬ Rubens, *The Judgment of Paris*, c. 1636-1639

Rubens painted anything that would raise your pulse—battles, miracles, hunts, and, especially, fleshy women with dimples on all four cheeks. For instance, *The Judgment of Paris* (one of two versions by Rubens in this museum) is little more than an excuse for a study of the female nude, showing front, back, and profile all on one canvas.

▸ *Next door in Room 22 is work by the great master of dramatic lighting, Rembrandt.*

### ⑭ Rembrandt, *Self-Portrait at the Age of 63*, 1669

Rembrandt throws the light of truth on...himself. He made this craggy self-portrait in the year he would die, at age 63. The greatest Dutch painter, he started out as the successful, wealthy young genius of the art world. But he refused to crank out commercial works. Rembrandt painted things that he believed in but no one would invest in—family members, down-to-earth Bible scenes, and self-portraits like this one.

Here, Rembrandt surveys the wreckage of his independent life. He was bankrupt, his mistress had just died, and he had also buried several of his children. We see a disillusioned, well-worn, but proud old genius.

▸ *Nearby, in Room 24, find...*

Rubens—dimpled-cheek Baroque excess  Rembrandt—proud self-portrait

## ⓯ Rembrandt, *Belshazzar's Feast*, c. 1635

Belshazzar, the wicked king of Babylon, has been feasting with God's sacred dinnerware when the meal is interrupted. The king turns to see the hand of God, burning an ominous message into the wall that Belshazzar's number is up. As he turns, he knocks over a goblet of wine.

Rembrandt captures the scene at the most ironic moment. Belshazzar is about to be ruined. We know it, his guests know it, and, judging by the look on his face, he's coming to the same conclusion.

Rembrandt's flair for the dramatic is accentuated by the strong contrast between the dark brown and bright light.

▶ *Enter Room 29 and exit at the far end. In Room 30 (with red wallpaper), on the left-hand wall, you'll find...*

## ⓰ Velázquez, *The Rokeby Venus*, c. 1647-1651

Like a Venetian centerfold, Venus lounges diagonally across the canvas, admiring herself, with flaring red, white, and gray fabrics to highlight her rosy white skin and inflame our passion. Horny Spanish

Rembrandt—Belshazzar's uh-oh moment

kings loved Titianesque nudes despite Spain's strict Inquisition, the Church tribunal that rooted out bad behavior. This work by the king's personal court painter is a rare Spanish nude from that ultra-Catholic country. The sole concession to Spanish modesty is the false reflection in the mirror—if it really showed what the angle should show, Velázquez would have needed two mirrors...and a new job.

▶ *From Room 30, turn left into the big, red Room 31, where you'll see a large canvas.*

## ⑰ Van Dyck, *Equestrian Portrait of Charles I*, c. 1637-1638

King Charles sits on a huge horse, accentuating his power. The horse's small head makes sure that little Charles isn't dwarfed. Charles was a soft-on-Catholics king in a hardcore Protestant country until England's Civil War (1648), when his genteel head was separated from his refined body by Cromwell and company.

Kings and bishops used the grandiose Baroque style to impress the masses with their power. Van Dyck's portrait style set the tone for all the stuffy, boring portraits of British aristocrats who wished to be portrayed as sophisticated gentlemen—whether they were or not.

▶ *Return to Room 30 and turn left, exiting at the far end, and entering Room 32. On the right wall, find...*

## ⑱ Caravaggio, *The Supper at Emmaus*, 1601

After Jesus was crucified, he rose from the dead and appeared without warning to some of his followers. Jesus just wants a quiet meal, but the man in green, suddenly realizing who he's eating with, is about to jump out of his chair in shock.

Caravaggio exaggerated grittiness, using real, ugly, unhaloed

Velázquez's racy Venus

King Charles I, divine monarch

Caravaggio—saints as everyday people

Boucher—Pan seeks a threesome.

people in Bible scenes. His paintings look like how a wet dog smells. From the torn shirts to the five o'clock shadows, we are witnessing a very human miracle.

▶ *Leave Room 32 at the far end, and enter Room 33.*

## French Rococo (1700s)

As Europe's political and economic center shifted from Italy to France, Louis XIV's court at Versailles became its cultural hub. Every aristocrat spoke French, dressed French, and bought French paintings. The Rococo art of Louis' successors was as frilly, sensual, and suggestive as the decadent French court. We see their rosy-cheeked portraits and their fantasies: lords and ladies at play in classical gardens, where mortals and gods cavort together.

▶ *One of the finest examples is the tiny...*

### ⑲ Boucher, *Pan and Syrinx,* 1759

Curious Pan seeks a threesome, but to elude him, Syrinx eventually changes into reeds, leaving him all wet.

Rococo art is like a Rubens that got shrunk in the wash—smaller, lighter pastel colors, frillier, and more delicate than the Baroque style. Same dimples, though.

▶ *Enter Room 34. Take a hike around and enjoy the English country-garden ambience.*

## British Romantic Art (Early 1800s)

### ⑳ Constable, *The Hay Wain,* 1821

The reserved British were more comfortable cavorting with nature than with the lofty gods. John Constable set up his easel out-of-doors, making quick sketches to capture the simple majesty of billowing clouds, spreading trees, and everyday rural life. This simple style was considered shocking in its day, scandalizing art lovers used to the highfalutin, prettified sheen of Baroque and Rococo.

### ㉑ Turner, *The Fighting Téméraire*, 1839

During the Industrial Revolution, machines began to replace humans, factories belched smoke over Constable's hay cart, and cloud-gazers had to punch the clock. Alas, here a modern steamboat symbolically drags a famous but obsolete sailing battleship off into the sunset to be destroyed.

Turner's messy, colorful style gives us our first glimpse into the modern art world—he influenced the Impressionists. Turner takes an ordinary scene (like Constable), captures the play of light with messy paints (like Impressionists), and charges it with mystery (like, wow).

▸ *To view more work by Constable, Turner, and other Brits, visit London's Tate Britain. For now, enter Room 41.*

## Impressionism and Beyond (1850-1910)

For 500 years, a great artist was someone who could paint the real world with perfect accuracy. Then along came the camera, and, *click,* the artist was replaced by a machine. But unemployed artists refused to go the way of *The Fighting Téméraire.*

They couldn't match the camera for painstaking detail, but they could match it—even beat it—in capturing color, the fleeting moment, the candid pose, the play of light and shadow, the quick impression. A new breed of artists burst out of the stuffy confines of the studio. They donned scarves and berets and set up their canvases in farmers' fields or carried their notebooks into crowded cafés, dashing off quick sketches in order to catch a momentary...impression.

▸ *The Impressionist paintings are scattered throughout Rooms 41-46. Here are a few of my favorites. Start with...*

### ㉒ Monet, *The Water-Lily Pond*, 1899

In his Giverny home, near Paris, Claude Monet planned an artificial garden, rechanneled a stream, built a bridge, and planted water lilies. Various paintings in the Gallery collection show scenes from Monet's garden—an oasis of order and calm in a hectic world.

Renoir, *The Skiff*

### ㉓ Monet, *Gare St. Lazare,* 1877

Monet, the father of Impressionism, was more interested in the play of light off his subject than the subject itself. He uses smudges of white and gray paint to capture how sun filters through the glass roof of the train station and is refiltered through the clouds of steam.

▶ *Continue browsing Rooms 41-46 to find work in the Impressionist and Post-Impressionist styles.*

### ㉔ Manet, *Corner of a Café-Concert,* 1878-1880

Imagine just how mundane (and therefore shocking) Manet's quick "impression" of this café must have been to a public that was raised on Greek gods, luscious nudes, and glowing Madonnas.

### ㉕ Renoir, *The Skiff,* 1875

Move in close. The "scene" breaks up into almost random patches of bright colors. The "blue" water is actually separate brushstrokes of blue, green, pink, purple, gray, and white. The rower's hat is a blob of green, white, and blue. Up close, it looks like a mess, but when you back

Seurat used lots of dots to "build" a scene.

up to a proper distance, *voilà!* It shimmers. This kind of rough, coarse brushwork (where you can actually see the brushstrokes) is one of the telltale signs of Impressionism. Renoir was not trying to paint the water itself, but the reflection of sky, shore, and boats off its surface.

### 26 Seurat, *Bathers at Asnières*, 1884

Viewed from about 15 feet away, this is a bright, sunny scene of people lounging on a riverbank. Up close it's a mess of dots. The "green" grass is a shag rug of green, yellow, red, brown, purple, and white brushstrokes. The boy's "red" cap is a collage of red, yellow, and blue.

▶ *Don't miss one of the don't-miss paintings here, which is usually in Room 43.*

### 27 Van Gogh, *Sunflowers*, 1888

In military terms, Van Gogh was the point man of his culture. He went ahead of his cohorts, explored the unknown, and caught a bullet young. He added emotion to Impressionism, infusing life even into inanimate objects. These sunflowers, painted with characteristic swirling brushstrokes, shimmer and writhe in either agony or ecstasy—depending on your own mood.

Van Gogh's *Sunflowers* bloom eternally.

Cézanne bridges Impressionism and Cubism.

▶ *A good place to end your visit is at one of the museum's most modern works...*

## ㉘ Cézanne, *Bathers*, c. 1894-1905

These bathers are arranged in strict triangles à la Leonardo—the five nudes on the left form one triangle, the seated nude on the right forms another, and even the background trees and clouds are triangular patterns of paint.

Cézanne uses the Impressionist technique of building a figure with dabs of paint. But his "dabs" are often larger-sized "cube" shapes that helped inspire a radical new style—Cubism.

▶ *Our tour is over, and the 21st century beckons. Exiting Room 46, you find yourself in the stairwell of the Gallery's main entrance (under the dome) on Trafalgar Square. Another set of stairs nearby (look for signs) can lead you elsewhere in the building. Otherwise, step back outside into Trafalgar Square, where the National Portrait Gallery is just around the corner. You're in the heart of London, surrounded by a lifetime of sights yet to enjoy.*

# West End Walk

*From Leicester Square to Piccadilly Circus*

The West End, the area just west of the original walled City of London, is London's liveliest neighborhood. Here is where you'll feel the pulse of the living, breathing London of today. Theaters, pubs, restaurants, bookstores, international cuisine, markets, and boutiques attract rock stars, punks, tourists, and ladies and gentlemen stepping from black cabs for a night on the town.

This two-hour walk samples the entertainment energy at Leicester Square, the festivity of Covent Garden, the rock-and-roll history of Denmark Street, the bohemian vibe of Soho, the shopping hustle and bustle of Carnaby and Regent Streets, and the neon hub of Piccadilly Circus.

# THE WALK BEGINS

Start at Leicester Square (Tube: Leicester Square). This walk is fun for sightseeing by day or nightlife after dark. Early evenings are ideal, since most pubs and squares are bubbling with locals enjoying a post-work pint or pre-theater bite.

▶ *Stand at the top of the square and take in the scene.*

## ❶ Leicester Square

Leicester (LESS-ter) Square is ground zero for London's entertainment. The square's **movie theaters**—the Odeon (Britain's largest cinema), Empire, and Vue—are famous for hosting red-carpet movie premieres. When Bradley Cooper, Benedict Cumberbatch, Keira Knightley, or Jennifer Lawrence need a publicity splash, it'll likely be here. (Search online for "London film premieres" to find upcoming events.) On any given night, this area is a mosh-pit of clubs and partying teens in town from the suburbs.

Leicester Square is the central clearinghouse for daytime theater ticket sales. Check out the **TKTS booth** and ignore all the other establishments that bill themselves as "half-price" (they're just normal booking agencies). It's often cheaper still to buy tickets directly from one of the theaters we'll pass on this walk.

Global Studios, former home of **Capital Radio London** (next to the Odeon), played a role in rock-and-roll history. Back in the 1960s, the BBC was the only radio station in town, and it was mostly talk and Bach, with a smattering of pop. The British Invasion was in full swing—The Beatles, The Rolling Stones, The Who—but Brits couldn't hear it. Rock fans had to resort to "pirate" radio stations, beamed from Luxembourg or from ships at sea. Finally, in 1973, Capital Radio was allowed to play rock music. Today, FM 95.8 carries on as a major top-40 broadcasting power.

▶ *Exit Leicester Square from its top corner, heading east (past the Vue cinema) on Cranbourn Street. Cross Charing Cross Road and continue along Cranbourn to the six-way intersection. Then, angle right onto Garrick Street. Shortly afterward, turn left onto calm, brick-lined Floral Street. At James Street, turn right and head for...*

## ❷ Covent Garden

Covent Garden (only tourists pluralize the name) is a large square teeming with people and street performers—jugglers, sword swallowers, magicians, and guitar players. London's buskers (including those in the Tube) are auditioned, licensed, and assigned times and places where they are allowed to perform.

The square's centerpiece is an iron-and-glass covered marketplace. A market has been here since medieval times, when it was the "convent" garden owned by Westminster Abbey. Covent Garden remained a produce market until 1973, when its venerable arcades were converted to boutiques, cafés, and antique shops.

Pan the square to find the world-class **Royal Opera House** (with a low-profile entrance in the northeast corner of the square) and the **London Transport Museum** (southeast corner). **St. Paul's Church** (not the famous cathedral) is to the west, with its Greek temple-like facade and blue clock face. St. Paul's is known as the Actors' Church, and its interior is lined with memorials to theater folk, some of whom (Chaplin, Karloff) you might recognize. The church is still a favorite of nervous performers praying for success.

▶ *Now browse your way northwest, along some lively and colorful streets.*

## ❸ From Covent Garden to Charing Cross Road

From Covent Garden, backtrack two blocks up James Street and continue straight up narrow Neal Street. Turn left on Short's Gardens, where Neal's Yard Dairy (at #17) sells a wide variety of cheeses from the British Isles and gives out samples if you ask nicely.

Continue along Short's Gardens to the next intersection—called

Leicester Square hosts red-carpet premieres.

Covent Garden—browsing the shops

# West End Walk

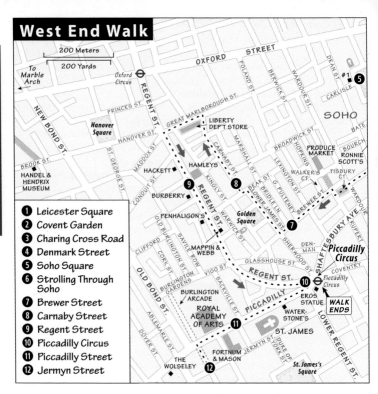

To Marble Arch

200 Meters
200 Yards

OXFORD STREET

Oxford Circus

SOHO

LIBERTY DEP'T STORE

HANOVER SQUARE

HANDEL & HENDRIX MUSEUM

HACKETT
HAMLEYS
PRODUCE MARKET
RONNIE SCOTT'S

BURBERRY
PENHALIGON'S

Golden Square

BURLINGTON ARCADE
MAPPIN & WEBB

Piccadilly Circus

REGENT ST.

EROS STATUE
WALK ENDS

PICCADILLY
WATER-STONE'S
ROYAL ACADEMY OF ARTS
ST. JAMES

THE WOLSELEY
FORTNUM & MASON
St. James's Square

1. Leicester Square
2. Covent Garden
3. Charing Cross Road
4. Denmark Street
5. Soho Square
6. Strolling Through Soho
7. Brewer Street
8. Carnaby Street
9. Regent Street
10. Piccadilly Circus
11. Piccadilly Street
12. Jermyn Street

**Seven Dials**—where seven sundials atop a pole mark the meeting of seven small streets. Built in 1694, this once served the timekeeping needs of this busy merchants' quarter. Continue straight ahead onto Earlham Street.

Then, bearing left, you'll spill out into **Cambridge Circus**—the busy intersection of Shaftesbury Avenue and Charing Cross Road—with its fine red-brick Victorian architecture and classic theaters. **Charing Cross Road** is the traditional home of London's bookstores.

▶ *Turn right up Charing Cross and walk two blocks to reach* **Foyles Books,** *which often hosts free book signings and jazz music (usually around 18:00 or 19:00, 107 Charing Cross Road, www.foyles.co.uk).*

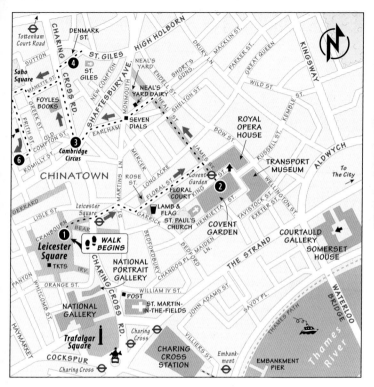

*A few steps up from Foyles, turn right onto...*

## ❹ Denmark Street

This seemingly nondescript little street is a musician's mecca. In the 1920s, it was known as "Britain's Tin Pan Alley"—the center of the UK's music-publishing industry, when songwriters here cranked out popular tunes printed as sheet music.

Later, in the 1960s, Denmark Street was the epicenter for rock and roll's British Invasion, which brought so much great pop music to the US. **Regent Sound Studio** (at #4, on the right) was a low-budget recording studio. Here, The Rolling Stones recorded "Not Fade Away."

Seven Dials intersection                    Denmark Street—home of British rock and roll

Other acts that recorded on Denmark Street include The Who ("Happy Jack"), The Kinks ("Denmark Street"), and The Beatles ("Fixing a Hole"). Today, Regent is a music store.

The **storefront** at #20 was formerly a music publishing house that employed a lowly office boy named Reginald Dwight. In 1969, on the building's rooftop, he wrote "Your Song" and went on to become famous as Sir Elton John. In the 1970s, the Sex Pistols lived in apartments above #6. The **12 Bar Café** at #25, on the left (now closed), helped launch the careers of more recent acts: Damien Rice, KT Tunstall, Jeff Buckley, and Keane.

Today, Denmark Street offers one-stop shopping for the modern musician. Without leaving this short street, you could buy a vintage Rickenbacker guitar, get your sax repaired, take piano lessons, lay down a bass track, have a few beers, or tattoo your name across your knuckles like Ozzy Osbourne.

▶ *From Denmark Street, go back across Charing Cross Road and head down Manette Street. After a short block, on the right (down the lane called Orange Yard) you'll see* **The Borderline,** *where R.E.M. and Oasis have played. Continue down Manette Street and under the "Pillars of Hercules" passage, then turn right up Greek Street to...*

## ❺ Soho Square

The Soho neighborhood is London's version of New York City's Greenwich Village. It's ritzy, raffish, edgy, and colorful. Having escaped modern urban development, it retains its quiet, residential, pedestrian-friendly feel.

Soho Square Gardens is a favorite place on a sunny afternoon.

The little house in the middle of the square is the gardener's hut. At #1, on the west (left) side of the square, the MPL building (McCartney Publishing Limited) houses offices of one of Britain's richest musicians, Sir Paul McCartney.

▶ *At the bottom of the square, exit down Frith Street. Stroll two blocks, enjoying the atmosphere as you make your way to the intersection with Old Compton Street.*

## ❻ Strolling Through Soho

The restaurants and boutiques here and on adjoining streets (such as Greek, Dean, and Wardour streets) are trendy and creative, the kind that attract high society when they feel like slumming it. Bars with burly, well-dressed bouncers abound. Private clubs cater to the late-night rock crowd.

**Ronnie Scott's Jazz Club** (at 47 Frith Street), has featured big-name acts for more than 50 years. In 1970, Jimi Hendrix jammed here in his last performance before his death a few days later. Even today Ronnie Scott's is *the* place to go for jazz in London.

Turn right on Old Compton Street. You're at the center of the neighborhood, surrounded by the buzz of Soho. Take in the eclectic variety of people going by. The many **rainbow flags** you see here recall a time when these streets were a center of London's LGBTQ scene.

At the corner of Old Compton and Dean Street, look left on Dean Street. The pagoda-style arch in the distance marks London's underwhelming **Chinatown,** with Gerrard Street as its spine.

▶ *Continue along Old Compton Street to where it squeezes down into a narrow alley (Tisbury Court). Penetrate this sleazy passage of sex shows and blue-video shops, tolerate the barkers' raunchy come-ons, then jog a half-block right and turn on Brewer Street.*

## ❼ Brewer Street: Sleaze, Porn Shops, and Prostitutes

Soho was a bordello zone in the 19th century. A bit of that survives today in this area. Sex shops, video arcades, and prostitution mingle with upscale restaurants here in west Soho. While it's illegal in Britain to sell sex on the street, well-advertised "models" entertain (profitably) in their tiny apartments.

One block north of Brewer Street—up Walker's Court—Berwick Street hosts a produce market (closed Sun).

Soho's Chinatown—less inviting than it looks

Soho—still some seediness amid the glitz

▶ *When you reach the intersection of Brewer Street and Sherwood Street (which is also called Lower James Street), turn right and walk two blocks north (on what is now called Upper James Street). Then jog left at Beak Street to find...*

## ❽ Carnaby Street

In the Swinging '60s, when Pete Townshend needed a paisley shirt, John Lennon a Nehru jacket, or Twiggy a miniskirt, they came here—where those mod fashions were invented. Today, there's not a hint of hippie. For the most part, Carnaby Street looks like everything else from the '60s does now—sanitized and co-opted by upscale franchises. At least the upper end of the street retains a whiff of funkiness.

▶ *Walk north the length of Carnaby Street, turn left on Great Marlborough Street, and head to Regent Street. You'll pass the venerable Liberty department store in the faux-Tudor building, known for its colorful "Liberty Print" fabrics. At Regent Street, begin strolling downhill.*

## ❾ Regent Street

You're in the heart of London's high-class, top-dollar shopping neighborhood. Regent Street has wide sidewalks and fine architecture, and most of the shops call the Queen their landlord, as she owns much of the land.

Just downhill from Liberty, follow the giddy kids to **Hamleys** (at #188), Britain's biggest toy store. It's been delighting children for more than 250 years. It was here that the world first got to know the Build-a-Bear workshop (now a fixture at malls everywhere) and Britain's

Regent Street bends with the latest fashion trends.

genteel Paddington Bear. Seven floors buzz with 50,000 toys, managed by a staff of 200. Employees, some dressed in playful costumes, give demos of the latest gadgets.

Continuing along the street, you'll pass fine bits of old English class. **Hackett** (across from Hamleys at #193) is the place to go for preppy young English menswear. **Mappin and Webb** (left, at #132) is the queen's jeweler. **Penhaligon's** (right, at #125) is the quintessential English perfumery, where royals shop for classic English scents like lavender and rose. **Burberry** (right, at #121) is a clothier of the royal family.

▶ *Regent Street arcs seductively into the ever-vibrant...*

## ⑩ Piccadilly Circus

London's most touristy square got its name from the fancy ruffled shirts—*picadils*—made in the neighborhood long ago. In the late 20th century, the square veered toward the gimmicky and tacky—look no further than the gargantuan Body Works exhibit.

In recent years, it's become more pedestrian-friendly. The tipsy

Piccadilly—Eros statue and neon ads    Beau Brummel welcomes gentlemen shoppers.

but perfectly balanced Eros statue marks the center of this people magnet. At night, when neon light pulses, 20-foot-high video ads paint the classic Georgian facades in a rainbow of colors. Black cabs honk, tourists crowd the attractions, and Piccadilly shows off big-city London at its glitziest.

► *Our walk is done. If you have more energy, you could head west down* ⓫ ***Piccadilly Street*** *to the Fortnum & Mason department store (#181), with its classy ambience and traditional afternoon tea. A half-block farther along Piccadilly Street, a left turn down the Piccadilly Arcade leads to quiet* ⓬ ***Jermyn Street.*** *A statue of Beau Brummell, the ultimate dandy, welcomes you to this neighborhood of clothing stores that have catered to upper-class gentlemen for generations. Pick up an elegant ascot or bowler hat, or head back to Piccadilly Square.*

# British Museum Tour

In the 19th century, the British flag flew over one-fourth of the world, and England collected art as fast as it collected colonies. The British Museum became the chronicle of Western civilization. It's the only place I can think of where you can follow the rise and fall of three great cultures in a few hours with a coffee break in the middle.

See pharaohs and their mummies from ancient Egypt, and the multilingual Rosetta Stone. From mighty Assyria come truck-sized statues and poignant scenes of hunted lions. The finale is the Elgin Marbles, the renowned sculptures that once decorated the Parthenon of Golden Age Greece. While the sun never set on the British Empire, it will set on you, so on this tour we'll see just the most exciting two hours.

# ORIENTATION

**Cost:** Free, £5 suggested donation. Interesting temporary exhibits usually require a separate admission (and a timed ticket).

**Hours:** Daily 10:00-17:30, Fri until 20:30 (not all galleries).

**Information:** Ticket desk tel. 020/7323-8181, www.britishmuseum.org.

**When to Go:** Rainy days, Sundays, and school holidays are most crowded; weekday late afternoons, especially on Fridays, are least crowded.

**Getting There:** The main entrance is on Great Russell Street. From the Tottenham Court Road Tube stop, take exit #2, walk straight ahead, and take the first right on Great Russell Street. The Holborn and Russell Square Tube stops are also nearby.

**Tours:** Free 40-minute EyeOpener tours focus on select rooms (daily 11:00-15:45, every 15 minutes). The £7 multimedia guide offers dial-up info on 200 objects, as well as several theme tours. You can also download my free 🎧 British Museum audio tour.

**Cloakroom:** £2 per item. Large backpacks must be checked.

**Eateries:** The self-service **$ Court Café** is on the Great Court ground

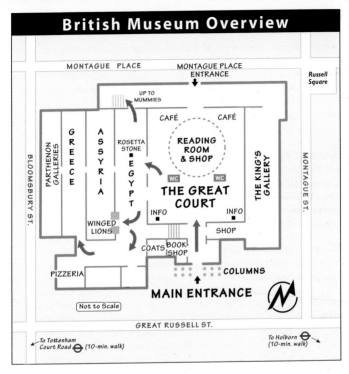

# British Museum Overview

MONTAGUE PLACE

MONTAGUE PLACE ENTRANCE

Russell Square

UP TO MUMMIES

CAFÉ    CAFÉ

GREECE

PARTHENON GALLERIES

ASSYRIA

ROSETTA STONE

EGYPT

READING ROOM & SHOP

WINGED LIONS

WC    WC

THE GREAT COURT

THE KING'S GALLERY

BLOOMSBURY ST.

MONTAGUE ST.

INFO    INFO

COATS

BOOK SHOP

SHOP

PIZZERIA

COLUMNS

Not to Scale

MAIN ENTRANCE

GREAT RUSSELL ST.

To Tottenham Court Road (10-min. walk)

To Holborn (10-min. walk)

floor. The **$$$ Court Restaurant** is on the upper level atop the Reading Room. The **$$ Pizzeria** is deeper into the museum, near the Greek art in Room 12. Nearby, there are lots of fast, cheap, and colorful cafés, pubs, and markets along Great Russell Street and Museum Street.

**Starring:** Rosetta Stone, Egyptian mummies, Assyrian lions, and the Parthenon sculptures.

# THE TOUR BEGINS

The main entrance on Great Russell Street spills you into the Great Court, a glass-domed space with the round Reading Room in the center (generally closed except for special exhibitions). From the Great Court, doorways lead to all wings. To the left are the exhibits on Egypt, Assyria, and Greece—our tour.

▶ *Enter the Egyptian Gallery. The Rosetta Stone is directly in front of you.*

## Ancient Egypt (3000 to 1000 BC)

Egypt was one of the world's first "civilizations"—a group of people with a government, religion, art, free time, and a written language. The Egypt we think of—pyramids, mummies, pharaohs, and guys who walk funny—lasted for 2,000 years with hardly any change in the government, religion, or arts.

### ❶ Rosetta Stone (196 BC)

When this rock was unearthed in the Egyptian desert in 1799, it was a sensation in Europe. This black slab caused a quantum leap in the study of ancient history. Finally, Egyptian writing could be decoded.

The hieroglyphic writing in the upper part of the stone was indecipherable for a thousand years. Did a picture of a bird mean "bird"? Or was it a sound, forming part of a larger word, like "burden"? As it turned out, hieroglyphics are a complex combination of the two, surprisingly more phonetic than symbolic. (For example, the hieroglyph that looks like a mouth or an eye is the letter "R.")

The Rosetta Stone allowed linguists to break the code. It contains

Rosetta Stone—inscribed in three languages

Ramesses II—a truck-sized statue fragment

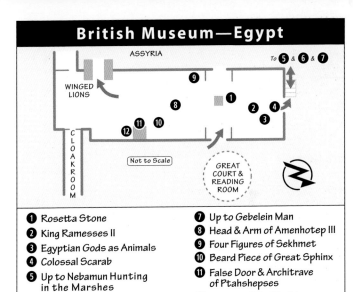

# British Museum—Egypt

ASSYRIA

To **5** & **6** & **7**

WINGED
LIONS

**9**

**8**        **1**

**2**  **4**

**11**  **10**        **3**

**12**

C
L
O
A
K
R
O
O
M

Not to Scale

GREAT
COURT &
READING
ROOM

**1** Rosetta Stone

**2** King Ramesses II

**3** Egyptian Gods as Animals

**4** Colossal Scarab

**5** Up to Nebamun Hunting
in the Marshes

**6** Up to Egyptian Funeral Objects

**7** Up to Gebelein Man

**8** Head & Arm of Amenhotep III

**9** Four Figures of Sekhmet

**10** Beard Piece of Great Sphinx

**11** False Door & Architrave
of Ptahshepses

**12** Statue of Nenkheftka

a single inscription repeated in three languages. The bottom third is plain old Greek (find your favorite frat or sorority), while the middle is medieval Egyptian. By comparing the two known languages with the one they didn't know, translators figured out the hieroglyphics.

The breakthrough came when they discovered that the large ovals (such as in the sixth line from the top) represented the name of the ruler, Ptolemy. Simple.

▶ *In the gallery to the right of the Stone, find the huge head of Ramesses.*

## **2** King Ramesses II (c. 1250 BC)

When Moses told the king of Egypt, "Let my people go!" this was the stony-faced look he got. Ramesses II ruled for 66 years (c. 1290-1223 BC) and may have been in power when Moses (as the Bible says) cursed Egypt with plagues, freed the Israeli slaves, and led them out of Egypt to their homeland in Israel.

This seven-ton statue, made from two colors of granite, is a

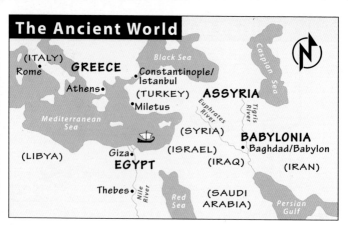

# The Ancient World

fragment from a temple in Thebes. It shows Ramesses with the traditional features of a pharaoh—goatee, cloth headdress, and cobra diadem on his forehead. Ramesses was a great builder of temples, palaces, tombs, and statues of himself. There are probably more statues of him in the world than there are cheesy fake *Davids*. He was so concerned about achieving immortality that he even chiseled his own name on other people's statues. Very cheeky.

▶ *Climb the ramp behind Ramesses, looking for animals.*

## ❸ Egyptian Gods as Animals

The Egyptians worshipped animals as incarnations of the gods. Though the displays here change, you may see the powerful ram—the god Amun (king of the gods)—protecting a puny pharaoh under his powerful chin. The falcon is Horus, the god of the living. The speckled, standing hippo (with lion head) is Taweret, protectress of childbirth. Finally, the cat (with ear- and nose-rings) served Bastet, the popular goddess of stress relief.

▶ *At the end of the Egyptian Gallery is a big stone beetle.*

## ❹ Colossal Scarab (c. 332 BC)

This species of beetle would burrow into the ground, then reappear—it's a symbol of resurrection, like the sun rising and setting, or death and rebirth. Scarab amulets were placed on mummies' chests

Scarab—beetle symbolizing rebirth

Nebamun—surprisingly realistic family scene

to protect the spirit's heart from acting impulsively. Pharaohs wore the symbol of the beetle, and tombs and temples were decorated with them (this one probably once sat in a temple). The hieroglyph for scarab meant "to come into being."

▶ *You can't call Egypt a wrap until you visit the mummies upstairs. Continue to the end of the gallery and up the West Stairs (four flights or elevator) to floor 3. Enter Room 61, with objects and wall paintings from the tomb of Nebamun.*

### ❺ Painting of Nebamun Hunting in the Marshes (c. 1350 BC)

Nebamun stands in a reed boat, gliding through the marshes. He raises his arm, ready to bean a bird with a snakelike hunting stick. On the right, his wife looks on, while his daughter crouches between his legs, a symbol of fatherly protection.

This nobleman walks like Egyptian statues look—stiff and flat, like he was just run over by a pyramid. We see the torso from the front and everything else—arms, legs, face—in profile, creating the funny walk that has become an Egyptian cliché.

But the stiffness is softened by a human touch. It's a family snapshot of loved ones. The only unrealistic element is the house cat (thigh-high, in front of the man) acting as a retriever—possibly the only cat in history that ever did anything useful.

When Nebamun passed into the afterlife, his awakening soul could look at this painting on the tomb wall and think of his loved ones for all eternity.

▶ *Browse through Rooms 62-63, filled with displays in glass cases.*

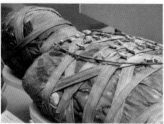

Mummy—preserving bodies for the afterlife          "Ginger"—5,400-year-old corpse

## ❻ Egyptian Funeral Objects

Mummifying a body is much like following a recipe. First, disembowel it (but leave the heart), then pack the cavities with pitch, and dry it with natron, a natural form of sodium carbonate (and, I believe, the active ingredient in Twinkies). Then carefully bandage it head to toe with hundreds of yards of linen strips. Let it sit 2,000 years, and...*voilà!*

The mummy was placed in a wooden coffin, which was put in a stone coffin, which was placed in a tomb. (The pyramids were super-sized tombs for the rich and famous.) The result is that we now have Egyptian bodies that are as well preserved as Larry King.

The internal organs were preserved alongside the mummy in canopic jars, and small-scale statuettes of the deceased (*shabtis*) were scattered around. Written in hieroglyphs on the coffins and the tomb walls were burial rites from the Book of the Dead. These were magical spells to protect the body and crib notes for the waking soul, who needed to know these passwords to get past the guardians of eternity.

Browse these rooms, noticing the Roman-era portraits of the deceased and the mummies of cats (Room 62). Worshipped in life as the sun god's allies, preserved in death, and memorialized with statues, cats were given the adulation they've come to expect ever since.

▶ *In Room 64, in a glass case, you'll find what's left of a visitor who tried to see it all...*

## ❼ Gebelein Man, Known as "Ginger"

This man died 5,400 years ago, a thousand years before the pyramids. His people buried him in the fetal position, where he could "sleep" for eternity. The hot sand naturally dehydrated and protected the body.

With him are a few of his possessions: bowls, beads, and the flint blade next to his arm. His grave was covered with stones. Named "Ginger" by scientists for his wisps of red hair, this man from a distant time seems very human.

▶ *Backtrack to Room 61 and head back down the stairs to the Egyptian Gallery and the Rosetta Stone. Just past the Rosetta Stone, find a huge head (facing away from you) with a hat like a bowling pin.*

## ❽ Head and Arm of a Statue of Amenhotep III (c. 1370 BC)

Art served as propaganda for the pharaohs, kings who called themselves gods on earth. Put this red-granite head on top of an enormous body (which still stands in Egypt), and you have the intimidating image of an omnipotent ruler who demands servile obedience. Next to the head is, appropriately, the pharaoh's powerful fist—the long arm of the law.

Amenhotep's crown is actually two crowns in one. The pointed upper half is the royal cap of Upper Egypt. This rests on the flat, fez-like crown symbolizing Lower Egypt. A pharaoh wearing both crowns together is bragging that he rules a combined Egypt.

▶ *Along the wall to the left of the red-granite head (as you're facing it) are four black lion-headed statues.*

## ❾ Four Figures of the Goddess Sekhmet (c. 1360 BC)

The lion-headed goddess Sekhmet looks pretty sedate here, but she could spring into a fierce crouch when crossed. She was the pharaoh's personal bodyguard, who could burn his enemies to a crisp with flaming arrows. Sekhmet holds an ankh. This key-shaped cross was the hieroglyph meaning "life" and was a symbol of eternal life. Later, it

Red Granite Head—fragment of a colossus

Sekhmet—the lion-headed goddess

was adopted as a Christian symbol because of its cross shape and religious overtones.

▶ *Continuing down the Egyptian Gallery, a few paces directly in front of you and to the left, find a glass case containing a...*

## ❿ Beard Piece of the Great Sphinx

The Great Sphinx—a statue of a pharaoh-headed lion—crouches in the shadow of the Great Pyramids in Cairo. Time shaved off the sphinx's soft, goatee-like limestone beard, and a piece is now preserved here in a glass case. This hunk of stone is only a whisker—about three percent of the massive beard—giving an idea of the scale of the six-story-tall, 250-foot-long statue.

▶ *Ten steps past the Sphinx's soul patch is a 10-foot-tall, red-tinted "building" covered in hieroglyphics.*

## ⓫ False Door and Architrave of Ptahshepses (c. 2400 BC)

This limestone "false door" was a ceremonial entrance (never meant to open) for a sealed building, called a *mastaba,* that marked the grave of a man named Ptahshepses. The hieroglyphs of eyes, birds, and rabbits serve as his epitaph, telling his life story: how he went to school with the pharaoh's kids, became an honored vizier, and married the pharaoh's daughter.

The deceased was mummified, placed in a wooden coffin that was encased in a stone coffin, then in a stone sarcophagus (like the **red-granite sarcophagus** in front of Ptahshepses' door), and buried 50 feet beneath the *mastaba* in an underground chamber.

*Mastabas* like Ptahshepses' were decorated inside and out with statues, steles, and frescoes like those displayed nearby. These pictured things that the soul would find useful in the next life—magical spells, lists of the deceased's accomplishments, snapshots of the deceased and his family while alive, and secret passwords from the Egyptian Book of the Dead. False doors like this allowed the soul (but not grave robbers) to come and go.

▶ *Just past Ptahshepses' false door is a glass case with a statue.*

## ⓬ Statue of Nenkheftka (c. 2400 BC)

Painted statues such as this one represented the soul of the deceased. Meant to keep alive the memory and personality of the departed, this image would have greeted Nenkheftka's loved ones when they brought

Limestone false door—spirits enter here.

Nenkheftka's soul takes a walk.

food offerings to place at his feet to nourish his soul. (In the mummification rites, the mouth was ritually opened, to prepare it to eat soul food.)

In ancient Egypt, you *could* take it with you. After death, your soul lived on, enjoying its earthly possessions—sometimes including servants, who might be walled up alive with their dead master. (Remember that even the great pyramids were just big tombs for Egypt's most powerful.)

Statues functioned as a refuge for the soul on its journey after death. The rich scattered statues of themselves everywhere, just in case. Statues needed to be simple and easy to recognize, mug shots for eternity: stiff, arms down, chin up, nothing fancy. This one has all the essential features, like the simplified human figures on international traffic signs. To a soul caught in the fast lane of astral travel, this symbolic statue would be easier to spot than a more detailed one.

With their fervent hope for life after death, Egyptians created calm, dignified art that seems built for eternity.

▶ *Relax. One civilization down, two to go. Near the end of the gallery, on the right, are two huge, winged Assyrian lions (with bearded human heads) standing guard over the Assyrian exhibit halls.*

## Ancient Assyria (c. 900-600 BC)
Long before Saddam Hussein, Iraq was home to other palace-building, iron-fisted rulers—the Assyrians.

Assyria was the lion, the king of beasts of early Middle Eastern civilizations. These Semitic people from the agriculturally challenged hills of northern Iraq became traders and conquerors, not farmers.

# British Museum—Assyria

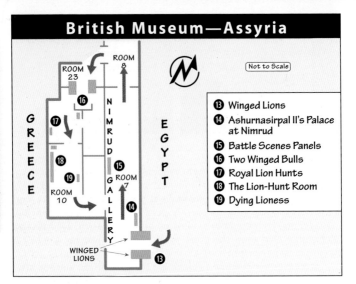

ROOM 8

ROOM 23

Not to Scale

GREECE

NIMRUD GALLERY

EGYPT

ROOM 7

ROOM 10

WINGED LIONS

⓭ Winged Lions
⓮ Ashurnasirpal II's Palace at Nimrud
⓯ Battle Scenes Panels
⓰ Two Winged Bulls
⓱ Royal Lion Hunts
⓲ The Lion-Hunt Room
⓳ Dying Lioness

They conquered their southern neighbors and dominated the Middle East for 300 years.

Their strength came from a superb army (chariots, mounted cavalry, and siege engines), a policy of terrorism against enemies ("I tied their heads to tree trunks all around the city," reads a royal inscription), ethnic cleansing and mass deportations of the vanquished, and efficient administration (roads and express postal service). They have been called the "Romans of the East."

## ⓭ Two Human-Headed Winged Lions (11th-8th century BC)

These stone lions guarded an Assyrian palace. With the strength of a lion, the wings of an eagle, the brain of a man, and the beard of an ancient hipster, they protected the king from evil spirits and scared the heck out of foreign ambassadors and left-wing newspaper reporters. (What has five legs and flies? Take a close look. These winged quintupeds, which appear complete from both the front and the side, could guard both directions at once.)

Carved into the stone between the bearded lions' loins, you can see one of civilization's most impressive achievements—writing. This wedge-shaped **(cuneiform)** script is the world's first written language, invented 5,000 years ago by the Sumerians (of southern Iraq) and passed down to their less-civilized descendants, the Assyrians.

▶ *Walk between the lions, glance at the large reconstructed wooden gates from an Assyrian palace, and turn right into the long, narrow red gallery (Room 7) lined with stone relief panels.*

## ⑭ Ashurnasirpal II's Palace at Nimrud (9th century BC)

This gallery is a mini version of the throne room and royal apartments of King Ashurnasirpal II's Northwest Palace at Nimrud. Entering, you'd see the king on his throne at the far end, surrounded by these pleasant, sand-colored, gypsum relief panels (which were, however, originally painted and varnished).

That's Ashurnasirpal himself in the **first panel on your right,** with braided beard, earring, and fez-like crown, flanked by his supernatural hawk-headed henchmen, who sprinkle incense on him with pinecones. The bulging forearms tell us that Ashurnasirpal II (r. 883-859 BC) was a conqueror's conqueror. The room's panels chronicle his bloody career.

▶ *A dozen paces farther down, on the left wall, are several relief panels (among many in this room that are worth focusing on).*

## ⑮ Panels with Battle Scenes

**Assyria at War:** The Assyrians lay siege with a crude "tank" that shields them as they smash down the gate with a battering ram. The king stands a safe distance away and bravely shoots arrows.

**Review of Prisoners:** Below the tank, prisoners are paraded before the Assyrian king, who is shaded by a parasol. Ashurnasirpal II

Assyrian winged lions standing guard

Assyrian king—a powerful conqueror

sneers and tells the captured chief, "Drop and give me 50." Above the prisoners' heads, we see the rich spoils of war—elephant tusks, metal pots, and so on.

**Crossing a River:** In another panel nearby, enemy soldiers flee the slings and arrows of outrageous Assyrians by swimming across the Euphrates, using inflated animal bladders as life preservers. Their friends (way downstream in the castle) applaud their ingenuity.

▸ *Exit the gallery at the far end, then hang a U-turn left. Pause at the entrance of Room 10c to see the impressive...*

## ⑯ Two Winged Bulls from the Palace of Sargon (c. 710-705 BC)

These marble bulls guarded the entrance to a vast palace complex built by Sargon II (r. 721-705 BC) near ancient Nineveh and Nimrud (today's Mosul). The 30-ton bulls were cut from a single block, tipped on their sides, then dragged to their place by POWs. (In modern times, when the British transported them here, they had to cut them in half; you can see the horizontal cracks through the bulls' chests.)

Sargon II gained his reputation as a general by subduing the Israelites after a three-year siege of Jerusalem (2 Kings 17:1-6). He solidified his conquest by ethnically cleansing the area and deporting many Israelites (inspiring legends of the "Lost" Ten Tribes).

▸ *Sneak between these bulls and veer right (into Room 10), where horses are being readied for the big hunt.*

## ⑰ Royal Lion Hunts from the North Palace of Ashurbanipal

On the right wall are horses; on the left are the hunting dogs. And next to them, lions, resting peacefully in a garden, unaware that they will shortly be rousted, stampeded, and slaughtered.

Lions lived in Mesopotamia up until modern times, and it was the king's duty to keep the lion population down to protect farmers and herdsmen. This duty soon became sport, with staged hunts and zoo-bred lions, as the kings of men proved their power by taking on the king of beasts.

▸ *Continue ahead into the larger lion-hunt room. Reading the panels like a comic strip, start on the right and gallop counterclockwise.*

## ⑱ The Lion-Hunt Room (c. 650 BC)

In these panels, the king's men release lions from their cages, then riders on horseback herd them into an enclosed arena. The king has them cornered. Having left a half-dozen corpses in his wake, he moves on, while spearmen hold off lions attacking from the rear.

▶ *At about the middle of the long wall...*

The fleeing lions, cornered by hounds, shot through with arrows, and weighed down by fatigue, begin to fall. The lead lion carries on even while vomiting blood.

▶ *On the wall opposite the vomiting lion is the...*

## ⑲ Dying Lioness

A lion roars in pain and frustration. She tries to run, but her body is too heavy. Her muscular hind legs, once a source of power, are now paralyzed. Like these brave, fierce lions, Assyria's once-great warrior nation was slain. A generation after these panels were carved, Assyria was conquered, and its capital at Nineveh was sacked and looted (612 BC). The mood of tragedy, dignity, and proud struggle in a hopeless cause makes this dying lioness one of the most beautiful of human creations.

▶ *Exit the lion-hunt room at the far end. Make your way back to the*

Dying lioness—tragic art of a dying civilization

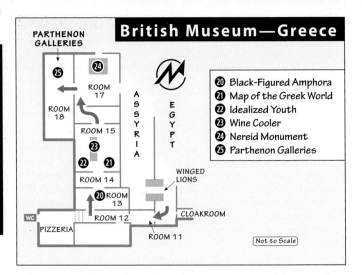

PARTHENON
GALLERIES

ROOM 17
ROOM 18
ROOM 15
ROOM 14
ROOM 13
ROOM 12
PIZZERIA
WC
ROOM 11
CLOAKROOM
WINGED LIONS
ASSYRIA
EGYPT

**20** Black-Figured Amphora
**21** Map of the Greek World
**22** Idealized Youth
**23** Wine Cooler
**24** Nereid Monument
**25** Parthenon Galleries

Not to Scale

*huge, winged lions who welcomed you to Assyria. Exit between them and make a U-turn to the right. Pass through Rooms 11-12 and turn right (if you're hungry, you can go straight to the Pizzeria) into Room 13, filled with Greek vases in glass cases.*

## Ancient Greece (600 BC–AD 1)

During its Golden Age (500-430 BC), Greece set the tone for all of Western civilization to follow. Democracy, theater, literature, mathematics, philosophy, science, gyros, art, and architecture as we know them, were virtually all invented by a single generation of Greeks in a small town of maybe 80,000 citizens.

▶ *In Room 13 is a Z-shaped glass case marked #8. It contains an item marked #231.*

## 20 Black-Figured Amphora with
## Achilles Killing Penthesilea (540-530 BC)

Greeks poured wine from jars like this one, which is painted with a legend from the Trojan War. On the vessel, Achilles of Greece faces off against the Queen of the Amazons, Penthesilea. (Achilles bears down, plunging a spear through her neck, as blood spurts. In her

Achilles exchanges meaningful eye contact.

Wine cooler—Greeks valued balanced art

dying moment, Penthesilea looks up, her gaze locking on Achilles. His eyes bulge wide, and he falls instantly in love with her. She dies, and Achilles is smitten.

▶ *Continue to Room 15. On the entrance wall, find a...*

### ㉑ Map of the Greek World (520-430 BC)

After Greece drove out Persian invaders in 480 BC, the city of Athens became the most powerful of the city-states and the center of the Greek world. A century after the Golden Age, Greek culture was spread still farther by Alexander the Great, who conquered the Mediterranean world and beyond (including Persia). By 300 BC, the "Greek" world stretched from Italy and Egypt to India. Two hundred years later, this Greek-speaking Hellenistic Empire was conquered by the Romans.

▶ *Find the nude male statue on the left side of the room.*

### ㉒ Torso of an Idealized Youth (Kouros, c. 520-510 BC)

The Greeks saw their gods in human form...and human beings were godlike. This youth exemplifies the divine orderliness of the universe with his once perfectly round head (now missing), symmetrical pecs, and navel in the center. The ideal man was geometrically perfect, a balance between movement and stillness, between realistic human anatomy (with human flaws) and the perfection of a Greek god. Our youth is still a bit uptight, stiff as the rock from which he's carved. But—as we'll see—in just a few short decades, the Greeks would cut loose and create realistic statues that seemed to move like real humans.

▶ *Two-thirds of the way down Room 15 (on the left) is a glass case containing a vase, labeled...*

Nereid Monument—a mini-Parthenon with similar features: pediment, frieze, and metopes

### ㉓ Wine Cooler Signed by Douris as Painter (490 BC)

This clay vessel, called a *psykter,* would have been topped off with wine and floated in a bowl of cooling water. Its red-figure drawings show satyrs at a *symposium* (drinking party). These half-man/half-animal creatures (notice their tails) had a reputation for lewd behavior, reminding the balanced and moderate Greeks of their rude roots.

The reveling figures painted on this jar are realistic, three-dimensional, and fluid. The art, like life, is more in balance. And speaking of "balance," if that's a Greek sobriety test, revel on.

▶ *Carry on into Room 17 and sit facing the Greek temple at the far end.*

### ㉔ Nereid Monument (c. 390-380 BC)

Greek temples (like this reconstruction of a temple-shaped tomb from Xanthos) were considered homes for the gods, with a statue of a god or goddess inside.

The triangle-shaped space above the columns—the pediment—is filled with sculpture. Supporting the pediment are decorative relief panels, called metopes. Now look through the columns to the building

# British Museum—Parthenon Galleries

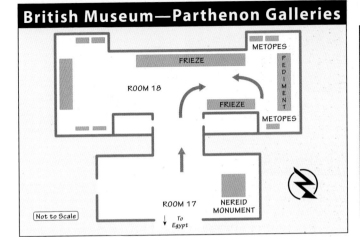

itself. Above the doorway, another set of relief panels—the frieze—runs around the building (under the eaves).

Next, we'll see pediment, frieze, and metope decorations from Greece's greatest temple.

▶ *Head through the glass doors labeled Parthenon Galleries. (The rooms branching off the entryway usually have helpful exhibits that reconstruct the Parthenon and its once-colorful sculptures.)*

## ㉕ Parthenon Galleries (447-432 BC)

The Parthenon—the temple dedicated to Athena, goddess of wisdom and the patroness of Athens—was the crowning glory of an enormous urban-renewal plan during Greece's Golden Age. After Athens was ruined in a war with Persia, the newly built Parthenon became the symbol of the Golden Age—a model of balance, simplicity, and harmonious elegance. Phidias, the greatest Greek sculptor, decorated the exterior with statues and relief panels.

While the building itself remains in Athens, many of the Parthenon's best sculptures are right here in the British Museum—the so-called Elgin Marbles, named for the shrewd British ambassador who had his men hammer, chisel, and saw them off the Parthenon in the early 1800s. Though the Greek government complains about losing

The Parthenon temple in Athens

Elgin Marbles—stripped from the Parthenon

its marbles, the Brits feel they rescued and preserved the sculptures. The often-bitter controversy continues.

The marble panels you see lining the walls of this large hall are part of the frieze that originally ran around the exterior of the Parthenon, under the eaves. The statues at either end of the hall once filled the Parthenon's triangular-shaped pediments. Near the pediment sculptures, we'll also find the relief panels known as metopes.

**The Frieze:** These 56 relief panels show Athens' "Fourth of July" parade, celebrating the birth of the city. On this day, citizens marched up the Acropolis to symbolically present a new robe to the 40-foot-tall, gold-and-ivory statue of Athena housed in the Parthenon.

▶ *Start at the panels by the entrance* **(#136),** *and work counterclockwise.*

Men on horseback lead the parade, all heading in the same direction—uphill. Prance on.

Notice the muscles and veins in the horses' legs and the intricate folds in the cloaks and dresses. Some panels have holes drilled in them, where gleaming bronze reins were fitted to heighten the festive look. All of these panels were originally painted in realistic colors. As you move along, notice that, despite the bustle of figures posed every which way, the frieze has one unifying element—all the people's heads are at the same level, creating a single ribbon around the Parthenon.

▶ *Cross to the opposite wall.*

A two-horse chariot **(#67),** cut from only a few inches of marble, is more lifelike and three-dimensional than anything the Egyptians achieved in a freestanding statue.

Enter the girls (five yards to the left, **#61**), the heart of the procession. Dressed in pleated robes, they shuffle past the parade marshals,

Pediment—the gods lounge to the left...          ...and right of Athena's amazing birth

carrying incense burners and jugs of wine and bowls to pour out an offering to the thirsty gods.

The procession culminates (#35) in the presentation of the robe to Athena. A man and a child fold the robe for the goddess while the rest of the gods look on. Overseeing it all are Zeus and Hera (#29), the king and queen of the gods, seated, enjoying the fashion show and wondering what length hemlines will be this year.

▶ *Head for the set of pediment sculptures at the far right end of the hall.*

**The Pediment Sculptures:** These statues were originally nestled nicely in the triangular pediment above the columns at the Parthenon's main (east) entrance. The missing statues at the peak of the triangle once showed the birth of Athena. Zeus had his head split open, allowing Athena, the goddess of wisdom, to rise from his brain fully grown and fully armed, inaugurating the Golden Age of Athens.

The other gods at this Olympian banquet slowly become aware of the amazing event. Hebe, the cupbearer of the gods (tallest surviving fragment) runs to tell the others, her dress whipping behind her. The only one who hasn't lost his head is laid-back Dionysus (the cool guy farther left). He just raises another glass of wine to his lips. Over on the right, Aphrodite, goddess of love, leans back into her mother's lap. A chess-set horse's head screams, "These people are nuts—let me out of here!"

The scene had a message. Just as wise Athena rose above the lesser gods, who were scared, drunk, or vain, so would her city, Athens, rise above her lesser rivals.

This is amazing workmanship. Compare Dionysus, with his natural, relaxed, reclining pose, to all those stiff Egyptian statues standing

## Centaurs Slain Around the World

Dateline 500 BC— Greece, China, India: Man no longer considers himself an animal. Bold new ideas are exploding simultaneously around the world. Socrates, Confucius, Buddha, and others are independently discovering a nonmaterial, unseen order in nature and in man. They say man has a rational mind or soul. He's separate from nature and different from the other animals.

eternally at attention. Appreciate the folds of the clothes on the female figures. Even without their heads, these statues, with their detailed anatomy and expressive poses, speak volumes.

▶ *The metopes are the panels on the walls to either side. Start with the three South Metope panels on the right wall.*

**The Metopes:** The metopes depict the battle between humans and centaurs. Metaphorically, they tell the story of Greece's own struggle to rise above nomadic barbarism to the pinnacle of early Western civilization.

The humans have invited some centaurs—wild half-man/half-horse creatures—to a wedding feast. The centaurs, the original party animals, get too drunk and try to carry off the women. A battle ensues. In **#XXXI,** a centaur grabs a man by the throat while the man pulls his hair. In **#XXX,** the centaur does the hair-pulling, and begins to drive the man to his knees.

In #XXVIII, the centaurs take control of the party, as one rears back and prepares to trample the helpless man. The leopard skin draped over the centaur's arm roars a taunt. The humans lose face.

But the humans rally. To the left, in #XXVII, a centaur tries to run, but the man grabs him by the neck and raises his (missing) right hand to finish him off.

The centaurs have been defeated. Civilization has triumphed

Metope #XXXI—centaurs battle humans     #XXVII—humans rally, defeating the barbarians

over barbarism, order over chaos, and rational man over his half-animal alter ego.

Why are the Parthenon sculptures so treasured? The British of the 19th century saw themselves as the new "civilized" race, subduing "barbarians" in their far-flung empire. Maybe these carved stones made them stop and wonder—will our great civilization also turn to rubble?

▶ *Our tour is over, but of course there's much more to the British Museum. Pick up the map (£2 donation) to find the 2,000-year-old Lindow Man (Room 50), Anglo-Saxon treasures (Room 41), a Michelangelo sketch (Room 90), and the elegant Enlightenment Gallery (Room 1). Look for remnants of the sophisticated, exotic cultures of Asia and the Americas (North Wing) and Africa (lower floor)—all part of the totem pole of the human family.*

# British Library Tour

The British Empire built its greatest monuments out of...paper. At the British Library, you'll see some of the many documents—literary, historical, and musical—that changed the course of history.

These national archives of Britain include more than 150 million items, 380 miles of shelving, and the deepest basement in London. But everything that matters for our visit is in one delightful room, where we'll focus on the highlights. We'll stand before old maps, ancient Bibles, Leonardo da Vinci's notebooks, the works of Shakespeare, highlights of English Lit 101, the Magna Carta, and—ladies and gentlemen—The Beatles.

# ORIENTATION

**Cost:** Free (£5 suggested donation); admission charged for special exhibits.

**Hours:** Mon-Thu 9:30-20:00, Fri until 18:00, Sat until 17:00, Sun 11:00-17:00.

**Information:** Tel. 019/3754-6060, info tel. 020/7412-7676, www.bl.uk.

**Getting There:** It's at 96 Euston Road, a block west of Tube: King's Cross St. Pancras.

**Tours:** There are no guided tours or audioguides for the permanent collection. ∩ Download my free British Library audio tour.

**Length of This Tour:** Allow one hour.

**Services:** Free coat check and lockers (no large bags).

**Eating:** The **$$$** upper-level restaurant has good hot meals. The **$$** ground-floor café (sandwiches and drinks) is next to the vast and fun pullout stamp collection.

Newton statue at the entrance—a symbol of knowledge

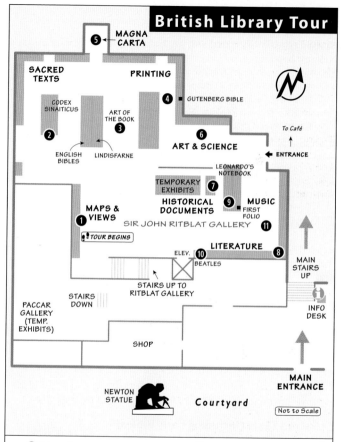

# British Library Tour

**5** MAGNA CARTA

**SACRED TEXTS**

**PRINTING**

CODEX SINAITICUS

**2**

ART OF THE BOOK **3**

**4** GUTENBERG BIBLE

ENGLISH BIBLES

LINDISFARNE

**ART & SCIENCE** **6**

To Café

← ENTRANCE

LEONARDO'S NOTEBOOK

TEMPORARY EXHIBITS **7**

**HISTORICAL DOCUMENTS**

**9** **MUSIC**

MAPS & VIEWS **1**

FIRST FOLIO

**11**

SIR JOHN RITBLAT GALLERY

TOUR BEGINS

**LITERATURE**

ELEV. **10** **8**

BEATLES

STAIRS UP TO RITBLAT GALLERY

MAIN STAIRS UP

PACCAR GALLERY (TEMP. EXHIBITS)

STAIRS DOWN

INFO DESK

SHOP

MAIN ENTRANCE

NEWTON STATUE

Courtyard

Not to Scale

---

**1** Maps & Views
**2** Sacred Texts & Early Bibles
**3** Art of the Book
**4** Printing
**5** Magna Carta
**6** Leonardo da Vinci's Notebook

**7** Historical Documents
**8** English Literature
**9** Shakespeare
**10** The Beatles
**11** Music

# THE TOUR BEGINS

Entering the library courtyard, you'll see a big statue of a naked Isaac Newton bending forward with a compass to measure the universe. The statue symbolizes the library's purpose: to gather all knowledge and promote humanity's endless search for truth.

Stepping inside, you'll find our tour in a single, dimly lit room to the left. It's variously labeled "The Sir John Ritblat Gallery," "Treasures of the British Library," or just "The Treasures."

▶ *Enter and let your eyes adjust. The room has display cases grouped according to themes: maps, sacred texts, music, and so on. Focus on the big picture, and don't be too worried about locating every specific exhibit in this tour—the displays change often. Start at the far side of the room with the display case of...*

## ❶ Maps and Views

These historic maps show how humans' perspective of the world has expanded over the centuries. These pieces of paper, encoded with information gleaned from travelers, could be passed along to future generations—each building upon the knowledge of the last.

You may see maps similar to these: A crude 13th-century map of Britain put medieval man in an unusual position—looking down on his homeland from 50 miles in the air. A few centuries later, maps of Britain were of such high quality they could be used today to plan a trip. And only a few generations after Columbus' first journey, the entire globe was fairly well-mapped, except for the mysterious expanse of unknown land that lay beyond America's east coast—"Terra Incognita."

▶ *Move into the area dedicated to sacred texts from several cultures.*

## ❷ Sacred Texts (Including Early Bibles)

Here the cases contain sacred texts such as the Hebrew Torah, Muslim Quran, Buddhist sutras, and Hindu Upanishads. You'll likely see some old decaying fragments of parchment or papyrus, with writing in ancient Latin, Greek, Egyptian, or other dead languages. These include some early bound books with pages, called a codex.

The **Codex Sinaiticus** (or the **Codex Alexandrinus** that may be

Lindisfarne Gospels—copied and illustrated by monks

on display instead) is one such bound book, from around AD 350. It's one of the oldest complete Bibles in existence.

Jesus didn't speak English, of course—nor did Moses or Isaiah or Paul or any other Bible authors or characters. Jesus spoke Aramaic, a form of Hebrew. His words were written down in Greek, decades after his death. Greek manuscripts were translated into Latin, the language of medieval monks and scholars. In the 1400s, English scholars began translating the Greek and Latin into the King's English. So our present-day English Bible is the fitful product of centuries of oral tradition, evolution, and translation. Today, Bible scholars pore diligently over every word from these earliest known versions of the Bible, trying to separate Jesus' authentic words from those that seem to have been added later.

There are several things that editors must do to compile the most "accurate" Bible: Decide which books actually belong, find the oldest and most accurate version of each book, and translate it correctly.

▶ *Nearby, you'll find more early Bibles (along with other texts) in the display cases called...*

### ❸ Art of the Book

After the fall of Rome, the Christian message was preserved by monks, who reproduced ancient Bibles by hand. The Bibles were often beautifully illustrated, or "illuminated."

The most magnificent of these medieval British "monk-uscripts" is the **Lindisfarne Gospels,** from AD 698. The text is in Latin, the language of scholars ever since the Roman Empire. The illustrations—with elaborate tracery and interwoven decoration—mix Irish, classical, and even Byzantine forms. (You can read an electronic copy of these manuscripts by using one of the touch-screen computers scattered around the room.)

These Gospels are a reminder that Christianity almost didn't make it in Europe. After the fall of Rome (which had established Christianity as the empire's official religion), much of Europe reverted to its pagan ways. Monasteries like the one at Lindisfarne (an island off the east coast of England) were the few beacons of light, tending the embers of civilization through the long night of the Dark Ages. While browsing the displays in Art of the Book (and in Sacred Texts), you'll likely see some **Early English Bibles.**

By the year 1400, the Bible was still written in Latin, even though only a small percentage of the population understood that language. A few brave reformers risked death to translate the sacred books into English. These Bibles were written in the same language you speak, but try reading them. The strange letters and archaic words clearly show how quickly languages evolve.

The King James version (made during his reign) has been the most widely used English translation. Fifty scholars worked for four years, borrowing heavily from previous translations, to produce this Bible. Its impact on the English language was enormous, making Elizabethan English something of the standard, even after people stopped saying "thee" and "thou" and "verily."

▶ *Move on to the wall of glass cases featuring early…*

## ❹ Printing

Printing was invented by the Chinese (what wasn't?). Printed **prayer sheets** were made using wooden blocks carved with Chinese characters, dipped into paint or ink, and pressed by hand onto the page.

The **Gutenberg Bible**—though it may look like just another monk-made Latin manuscript—was so revolutionary because it was the first book printed in Europe using movable type (c. 1455).

Here's how it works: You scratch each letter onto a separate metal block, then arrange them into words, ink them up, and press them onto paper. When one job was done you could reuse the same letters for a new one.

Suddenly, the Bible was available for anyone to read, fueling the Protestant Reformation. Knowledge became cheap and accessible to

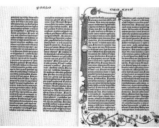

Gutenberg's press put monks out of work.

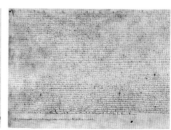

The Magna Carta established "due process."

a wide audience, not just the rich. Books became the mass medium of Europe, linking people by a common set of ideas.

▶ *Through a nearby doorway is a small room with the...*

## ❺ Magna Carta

How did Britain, a tiny island with a few million people, come to rule a quarter of the world? Not by force, but by law. The 1215 Magna Carta was the basis for England's constitutional system of government. Though historians talk about *the* Magna Carta, several different versions of the document exist, some of which are kept in this room.

In 1215, England's barons rose in revolt against the slimy King John. After losing London, John was forced to negotiate. The barons presented him with a list of demands (Articles of the Barons; labeled *King John*). John, whose rule was worthless without the barons' support, had no choice but to acquiesce and affix his seal to it. Some 35 copies of the final version of the "Great Charter" were distributed around the kingdom.

This was a turning point in the history of government. Now, for the first time, there were limits—in writing—on how a king could treat his subjects. More generally, it established the idea of "due process"—the notion that a government can't infringe on citizens' freedom without a legitimate legal reason. This small step became the basis for all constitutional governments, including yours.

So what did this radical piece of paper actually say? Not much. The specific demands were trivial by today's standards—the king's duties to widows and orphans, inheritance taxes, and so on. But the principle—that the king had to abide by them as law—was revolutionary.

▶ *Now return to the main room to find display cases featuring...*

## ❻ Art and Science

As books spread secular knowledge, Renaissance men turned their attention away from heaven and toward the nuts and bolts of the material world around them. Pages from **Leonardo da Vinci's notebook** show his powerful curiosity, his genius for invention, and his famous backward and inside-out handwriting, which makes sense only if you know Italian and have a mirror. Leonardo's restless mind pondered diverse subjects, from how birds fly, to the flow of the Arno River, to

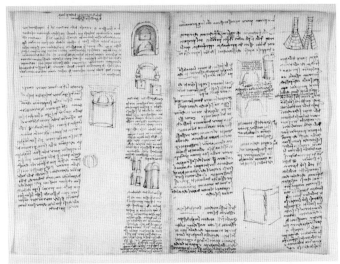

Leonardo's notebook: You'd need a mirror to read the ingenious inventor's backward writing.

military fortifications, to an early helicopter, to the "earthshine" reflecting onto the moon.

One person's research inspired another's, and books allowed knowledge to accumulate. Leonardo inspired Galileo, who championed the counter-commonsense notion that the earth spun around the sun. Galileo inspired Isaac Newton, who perfected the mathematics of those moving celestial bodies.

## ❼ Historical Documents
Nearby are many more historical documents. You may see letters by Henry VIII, Queen Elizabeth I, Darwin, Freud, Gandhi, and others. But for now, let's trace the evolution of...

## ❽ English Literature
Ponder the first English literary masterpiece, ***Beowulf.*** The manuscript is from AD 1000, although the story itself dates to about 750. In this Anglo-Saxon epic poem, the young hero Beowulf defeats two

half-human monsters threatening the kingdom. Beowulf symbolizes England's emergence from the chaos and barbarism of the Dark Ages.

Look for **The Canterbury Tales.** Geoffrey Chaucer's bawdy collection of stories (c. 1410), told by pilgrims on their way to Canterbury, gives us the full range of life's experiences—happy, sad, silly, sexy, and devout. While most serious literature of the time was written in scholarly Latin, the stories in *The Canterbury Tales* were written in Middle English, the people's tongue.

This display is often a greatest-hits sampling of literature in English, from Brontë to Kipling to Woolf to Joyce to Dickens, whose novels were as popular in his time as blockbuster movies are today. Works by contemporary writers show that Britain continues to be a powerful force in the world of ideas and imagination.

▶ *The most famous of England's writers generally gets his own display case.*

## ❾ Shakespeare

William Shakespeare is the greatest author in any language. Period. He expanded and helped define modern English. In one fell swoop, he made the language of everyday people as important as Latin. In the process, he gave us phrases like "one fell swoop," which we quote without knowing they're Shakespeare.

Perhaps as important was his insight into humanity. Think of his stock of great characters and great lines: Hamlet ("To be or not to be, that is the question"), Othello and his jealousy ("It is the green-eyed monster"), ambitious Mark Antony ("Friends, Romans, countrymen, lend me your ears"), rowdy Falstaff ("The better part of valor is discretion"), and the star-crossed lovers Romeo and Juliet ("But soft, what light through yonder window breaks"). Shakespeare probed the psychology of human beings 300 years before Freud. Even today, his characters strike a familiar chord.

Shakespeare wrote his plays to be performed, not read. He published a few, but as his reputation grew, unauthorized "bootleg" versions began to circulate. Some of these were written by actors who were trying (with faulty memories) to re-create plays they had appeared in years before.

It wasn't until seven years after his death, in 1623, that a nearly complete collection of Shakespeare's plays was published, commonly

BRITISH LIBRARY TOUR

Shakespeare, from the First Folio

Handel's *Messiah*

known as the **First Folio.** If the First Folio is not out for viewing, the library should have other Shakespeare items on display.

The engraving of Shakespeare on the title page is reportedly one of only two portraits done during his lifetime. Is this what he really looked like? No one knows. The best answer probably comes from Ben Jonson, in the introduction on the facing page. Jonson concludes, "Reader, look not on his picture, but his book."

▶ *Nearby are exhibits on music and...*

### ⑩ The Beatles

Bach, Beethoven, Brahms, Bizet...Beatles. Future generations will have to judge whether this musical quartet ranks with such artists, but no one can deny their historical significance. Look for photos of John Lennon, Paul McCartney, George Harrison, and Ringo Starr.

Among the displays, you may find manuscripts of song lyrics written by Lennon and McCartney, the two guiding lights of the group. "I Want to Hold Your Hand" was the song that launched them to superstardom in America. "A Hard Day's Night" and "Help" were title songs of two films capturing the excitement and chaos of their hectic touring schedule. Some call "Ticket to Ride" the first heavy-metal song. "Michelle," with a line in French, seemed oh-so-sophisticated. "Yesterday," by Paul, was recorded with guitar and voice backed by a string quartet—a touch of class from producer George Martin. Also, glance at the rambling, depressed, and cynical but humorous "untitled verse" by a young John Lennon. Is that a self-portrait at the bottom?

The Beatles captured the exuberant spirit of rebellious Baby Boomers across the globe.

## ⓫ Music

Kind of an anticlimax after the Fab Four, I know, but there are manuscripts by Mozart, Beethoven, Chopin, and others. George Frideric
Handel's famous oratorio, the **Messiah** (1741), is often on display. It
was written in a flash of inspiration—three hours of music in 24 days.
Here are the final bars of its most famous tune. Hallelujah.

# Tower of London Tour

William I, still getting used to his new title of "the Conqueror," built a castle tower here (1077-1097) to keep the Londoners in line. Over the centuries, his successors built more walls and towers around it to create this complex, which today covers 18 acres. The heavily fortified Tower served as a royal residence, the Royal Mint, the Royal Jewel House, and, most famously, as the prison and execution site of those who dared oppose the Crown.

The Tower represents the ultimate power of the monarch. See the execution site where Henry VIII axed exes. Ogle the crown jewels, the richest on earth. See prisons that held the likes of Sir Walter Raleigh, Queen Elizabeth, and the Nazi Rudolf Hess. Tour halls of armor and weapons and take a meaty Beefeater tour. You'll find more bloody history per square inch than anywhere else in Britain by touring this original tower of power.

**Cost:** £30.30, cheaper online, family ticket available.

**Hours:** Tue-Sat 9:00-17:30, Sun-Mon from 10:00; Nov-Feb closes one hour earlier.

**Information:** Tel. 0844-482-7788, www.hrp.org.uk.

**Advance Tickets:** To avoid long ticket-buying lines and save a few pounds, buy tickets in advance on the Tower website (print at home or collect at group ticket office—see map). Alternatively, you can buy a voucher at the Trader's Gate gift shop (look for blue awning down the stairway from the Tower Hill Tube stop). The voucher is good any day and can be exchanged for a ticket at the group ticket office.

**Avoiding Crowds:** It's most crowded in summer, on weekends (especially Sun), and during school holidays. Either arrive before 10:00 and go straight for the jewels, or come late and see the jewels an hour before closing time.

**Getting There:** The Tower is located in East London (Tube: Tower Hill). Thames Clippers boats make the trip between the Tower of London and Westminster Pier near Big Ben in 30-45 minutes.

**Yeoman Warder (Beefeater) Tours:** Free, worthwhile, one-hour Beefeater tours leave every 30 minutes from inside the entrance gate (last tour at 15:30—or 14:30 in Nov-Feb). The boisterous Beefeaters are great entertainers, whose historical talks include lots of bloody anecdotes and corny jokes.

**Length of This Tour:** Allow two hours.

**Eating:** The **$$** New Armouries Café, inside the Tower, is a big, efficient cafeteria. Outside the Tower, there's a row of chain eateries along the river and behind the Welcome Centre, and various takeout stands. Picnicking is allowed on Tower grounds.

**Starring:** The crown jewels, Beefeaters, William the Conqueror, and Henry VIII.

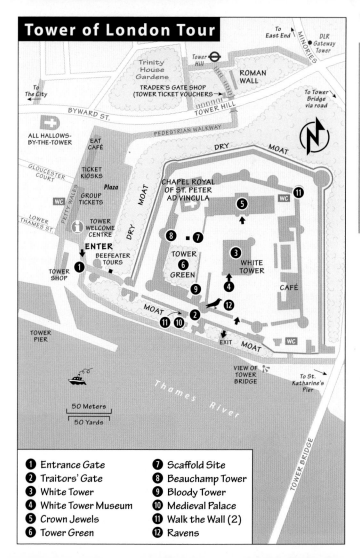

# THE TOUR BEGINS

## ❶ Entrance Gate

Even an army the size of the ticket line couldn't storm this castle. After the drawbridge was pulled up and the iron portcullis slammed down, you'd have to swim a 120-foot moat; cross an island prowled by wild animals; then toss a grappling hook onto a wall and climb up while the enemy poured boiling oil on you. If you made it this far, you'd only be halfway there. You'd still have to swim a second moat (now the grassy parade ground we see today), then, finally, scale a second, higher wall. In all, the central keep (tower) was surrounded by two concentric rings of complete defenses. Yes, it was difficult to get into the Tower (if you were a foreign enemy)...but it was almost as impossible to get out (if you were an enemy of the state).

▸ *Consult the daily schedule, and consider catching a Beefeater tour. Continue through the inner gate, where a bookstore on the right hands out a free map. When you're all set, go 50 yards straight ahead to the...*

## ❷ Traitors' Gate

This was the boat entrance to the Tower from the Thames. Princess Elizabeth, who was a prisoner here before she became Queen Elizabeth I, was carried down the Thames and through this gate on a barge, thinking about her mom, Anne Boleyn, who had been decapitated inside just a few years earlier. Many English leaders who fell from grace entered through here—Elizabeth was one of the lucky few to walk out.

▸ *Continue straight and turn left to pass underneath the archway just*

Some of the Tower's many ramparts

Traitors' Gate—the boat entrance

*before the cannons (opposite the exit), which leads into the inner court-
yard. The big, white tower in the middle is the...*

## ❸ White Tower

This square, 90-foot-tall tower is the original structure that gave this
castle complex its name. In the 13th century, the tower was painted
white (hence the name).

Standing high above the rest of old London, the White Tower pro-
vided a gleaming reminder of the monarchy's absolute power over its
subjects. If you made the wrong move here, you could be feasting on
roast boar in the Banqueting Hall one night and chained to the walls of
the prison the next. Torture ranged from stretching on the rack to the
full monty: hanging by the neck until nearly dead, then "drawing" (cut
open to be gutted), and finally quartering, with your giblets displayed
on the walls as a warning. Any cries for help were muffled by the thick
stone walls—15 feet at the base.

▶ *Either now or later, find time to go inside the White Tower for its excellent museum.*

## ❹ White Tower Museum

Inside the White Tower, a one-way route winds through exhibits re-
creating medieval life and the Tower's bloody history of torture and
executions.

The first suits of armor you see belonged to Henry VIII—on a
horse, slender in his youth (c. 1515), then more heavyset by 1540 (with
his bigger-is-better codpiece). Upstairs, the rare and lovely St. John's
Chapel (1080) is where Lady Jane Grey (described later) offered up a
last unanswered prayer. The Treasures of the Tower Armouries exhibit displays the heaviest suit of armor in the world (130 pounds!),
as well as weapons used through the ages, including machine guns
and the jeweled "Tiffany Revolver." On the top floor: There it is—the
Tower's actual chopping block and execution ax.

▶ *Back outside, get in the line straight ahead leading to the crown jewels. The queue is still quite long even once you've made it in the door,
but great videos help pass the time. They show close-ups of the jewels
and how they've been used during centuries of coronations, including
Queen Elizabeth II's in 1953. After passing a hallway of ceremonial
maces, swords, and trumpets, you finally reach the...*

The White Tower—the oldest of the Tower's towers—stands in the middle of the walled complex.

## The Beefeaters

The original duty of the Yeoman Warders (called "Beefeaters") was to guard the Tower,
its prisoners, and the jewels.
Their nickname may come
from an original perk of the
job—large rations of the king's
beef. The Beefeaters dress in
blue knee-length coats with
red trim and a top hat. The
"ER" on the chest stands for the monarch they serve—Queen Elizabeth
II (Elisabetha Regina in Latin). On special occasions, they wear red.
All are retired noncommissioned officers from the armed forces with
distinguished service records (and all were men until 2007).

These days, the 38 Yeoman Warders are entertaining tour guides.
They and their families make up the Beefeating community that live
inside the Tower.

### ❺ Crown Jewels

The first displays show the royal regalia. The monarch-to-be is
anointed with holy oil poured from the eagle-beak flask, dressed in
the 20-pound gold robe, and handed the jeweled sword. The 12th-
century coronation spoon, last used in 1953 to anoint the head of
Queen Elizabeth, is the most ancient object here. Most of the original
crown jewels from medieval times were lost during Cromwell's 1648
revolution. After being dressed and anointed, the new monarch prepares for the "crowning" moment.

▶ *Five glass cases display the various crowns, orbs, and scepters used in
royal ceremonies. Ride the moving sidewalk that takes you past them.
You're welcome to circle back and glide by again, or hang out on the
elevated viewing area. The displays change often, but the following
items are generally viewable.*

**Scepter and Orb:** After being crowned, the new monarch is
handed these items. The Sovereign's Scepter is encrusted with the
world's largest cut diamond—the 530-carat Star of Africa, beefy as a
quarter-pounder. This was one of nine stones cut from the original

Prisoners left pitiful messages.

The crown jewels

3,106-carat (1.37-pound) Cullinan diamond. The orb symbolizes how Christianity rules over the earth, a reminder that even a "divine monarch" is not above God's law.

**St. Edward's Crown:** On coronation day in Westminster Abbey, the archbishop places this crown upon the head of the new monarch. It's worn for 20 minutes, then locked away until the next coronation. The original crown, destroyed by Cromwell, was older than the Tower itself and dated back to 1061, the time of King Edward the Confessor, "the last English king" before William the Conqueror invaded from France (1066). This 1661 remake is said to contain some of the original's gold amid its 443 precious and semiprecious stones. Because the crown weighs nearly five pounds, weak or frail monarchs have opted not to wear it.

**Other Crowns:** Among the several crowns, notice how four-arch crowns are for monarchs, while princes get only two. **The Crown of the Queen Mother** has the 106-carat Koh-I-Noor diamond glittering on the front. The **Queen Victoria Small Diamond Crown** is tiny, because it was designed to sit atop Victoria's widow's veil. The impressive **Imperial State Crown** is what the Queen wears for official functions. It's the crown depicted on Britain's coins and stamps. Among its 3,733 jewels are Queen Elizabeth I's former earrings (the hanging pearls, top center) and a blue sapphire (on top) from the ring of King Edward the Confessor.

▸ *Leave the jewels by exiting through the thick vault doors, turn right, and proceed to the grassy field. This is...*

## ❻ Tower Green

This spacious courtyard within the walls was once the "town square" for those who lived in the castle. Knights exercised and jousted here, residents worshipped at the stone Chapel Royal of St. Peter ad Vincula ("in Chains"; north side), and this was the last place of refuge in troubled times. The Tower is still officially a royal residence: The Queen's lodgings are on the south side of the green, in the white half-timbered buildings where a soldier stands guard.

▶ *Near the middle of Tower Green is a granite-paved square marked* Site of Scaffold.

## ❼ Scaffold Site

The Tower's execution site looks pleasant enough today; the actual chopping block has been moved inside the White Tower, and a modern sculpture encourages visitors to ponder those who died.

Here, enemies of the Crown would kneel before the king for the final time. With their hands tied behind their backs, they would say a final prayer, then lay their heads on a block, and—*shlit*—the blade would slice through their necks, their heads tumbling to the ground. The headless corpses were buried in unmarked graves in Tower Green (to avoid becoming a shrine for their supporters) or under the floor of the Chapel Royal of St. Peter ad Vincula. The heads were stuck on a stick and displayed at London Bridge. Passersby did not really see the heads—they saw grotesque spheres of insects and parasites.

Tower Green was the most prestigious execution site at the Tower. Common criminals were hanged outside the Tower. More prominent evil-doers were decapitated before jeering crowds atop

The White Tower Museum displays armaments.

The executioner's ax

Tower Green—the complex's courtyard

Execution site—Anne Boleyn died here.

Tower Hill (near today's Tube station). Execution inside the Tower walls was reserved for the most heinous traitors.

Henry VIII axed a couple of his ex-wives here. Anne Boleyn was the appealing young woman Henry had fallen so hard for that he broke with the Catholic Church in order to divorce his first wife and marry her. But when Anne failed to produce a male heir, the court turned against her. She was locked up in the Tower, branded an adulteress and traitor, and decapitated.

Henry's fifth wife, teenage Catherine Howard, was also beheaded here. So was Jane Boleyn (Anne's sister-in-law) for arranging Catherine's adulterous affair behind Henry's back. Next.

The most tragic victim was 17-year-old Lady Jane Grey, who had been manipulated into claiming the Crown. When Bloody Mary (Mary I, Henry's daughter) took control, she forced her Protestant cousin Jane to kneel before the executioner. Young Jane bravely blindfolded herself, but then couldn't find the block. She crawled around the scaffolding pleading, "Where is it?!"

Years ago, a Beefeater, tired of the "Hollywood coverage" of the Tower, told me that in more than 900 years only 120 were executed here, and, of those, only 6 were executed inside the walls. Stressing the hospitality of the Tower, he added, "Torture was actually quite rare here."

▶ *Overlooking the scaffold site is the...*

## ❽ Beauchamp Tower

The Beauchamp Tower (pronounced "BEECH-um") was one of several places in the complex that housed Very Important Prisoners. In an upstairs room, you can read graffiti carved into the stone by bored and despondent inmates.

Picture Philip Howard, the Earl of Arundel (c. 1555-1595), warming himself by this fireplace and glancing out at the execution site during his 10-year incarceration. On June 22, 1587, he carved his family name "Arundell" into the chimney (graffiti #13) and wrote in Latin: "*Quanto plus afflictionis...*" ("The more we suffer for Christ in this world, the more glory with Christ in the next.")

Graffiti #85 belongs to Lady Jane Grey's young husband, Lord Guilford Dudley. Locked in the Beauchamp Tower and executed the same day as his wife, Dudley vented his despair by scratching "IANE" into the stone.

The last enemy of the state imprisoned in the Tower complex was one of its most infamous: the renegade Nazi Rudolf Hess. In 1941, Hitler's henchman secretly flew to Britain with a peace proposal (Hitler denied any such plan). He parachuted into a field, was arrested and held for four days in the Tower, and was later given a life sentence.

▶ *Back out on Tower Green, head down toward the river. At the bottom corner of the green is...*

## ❾ Bloody Tower

Not all prisoners died at the block. Sir Walter Raleigh—poet, explorer, and political radical—was imprisoned here for 13 years, accused of plotting against King James. While in prison, Raleigh wrote the first volume of his *History of the World*. Check out his rather cushy bedroom, study, and walkway (courtesy of the powerful tobacco lobby?). The 13-year-old King Edward V and his kid brother were kidnapped in 1483 during the Wars of the Roses by their uncle Richard III ("Now is the winter of our discontent...") and locked in the Bloody Tower, never to be seen again. End of story? Two centuries later, the skeletons of two unidentified children were found here.

▶ *Take the staircase down to the main entrance ramp (toward the river). Walk under the Bloody Tower, cross the cobbled road, and bear right a few steps to find the stairs up onto the wall.*

## ❿ Medieval Palace

The Tower was a royal residence as well as a fortress. These rooms were built around 1240 by Henry III, the king most responsible for

View of Tower (not "London") Bridge

A "knight" regales tourists near the ramparts.

the expansive Tower of London complex we see today. You'll see his re-created bedroom and throne room, both with massive fireplaces to keep this cold stone palace cozy.

▶ *From the throne room, continue up the stairs to...*

## ⓫ Walk the Wall

The Tower was defended by state-of-the-art walls and fortifications in the 13th century. This walk offers a good look. From the walls, you also get a fine view of the famous **Tower Bridge** straddling the Thames, with the twin towers and blue spans. Although it looks somewhat medieval, this drawbridge was built in 1894, of steel and concrete. Sophisticated steam engines raise and lower the bridge, allowing tall-masted ships to squeeze through.

Gaze out at the bridge, the river, City Hall (the egg-shaped glass building across the river), the Shard (London's bold exclamation point), and life-filled London.

▶ *Between the White Tower and the Thames are cages housing the...*

## ⓬ Ravens

According to goofy tradition, the Tower and the British throne are only safe as long as ravens are here. These eight impressive birds have clipped wings to keep them close. World War II bombing raids reduced the population to one. Some years ago, with their clipped wings, the birds had trouble mating, so a slide was built to help them get a bit of lift to facilitate the process. Happily, that worked, and a baby raven was born.

▶ *Take one final look at the stern stone walls of the Tower. Be glad you can leave.*

# Sights

London offers more world-class sights and museums than anyone could see in a single visit. To help you prioritize your limited time and money, I've clustered London's top sights into walkable neighborhoods for more efficient sightseeing. In the Westminster neighborhood, for example, you could string together a great day of sightseeing, linking Big Ben, Westminster Abbey, the Churchill War Rooms, and much more. You'll find a full day's worth of sights in the West End, The City, the South Bank, and other neighborhoods.

Remember that some of London's biggest sights (marked with a 🕮) are described in detail in the individual walks and tours chapters. A 🎧 means the sight is available as a free audio tour (via my Rick Steves Audio Europe app—see page 10). See the Practicalities chapter for sightseeing tips. Finally, remember that although sights can be crowded and stressful, London is all about gentility and grace. Be flexible.

# CENTRAL LONDON

## Westminster

In the shadow of Big Ben and Parliament, the Westminster neighborhood is Britain's government center. Most tourist sights lie in a half-mile stretch between Big Ben/Parliament (Tube: Westminster) and Trafalgar Square (Tube: Charing Cross).

### ▲▲▲Westminster Abbey

The greatest church in the English-speaking world, Westminster Abbey is where England's kings and queens have been crowned and buried since 1066.

 📖 See the Westminster Abbey Tour chapter.

### ▲▲Big Ben and the Houses of Parliament (Palace of Westminster)

This icon of London is where the British government's legislative branch meets. Big Ben, the 315-foot-high clock tower at the north end of the Houses of Parliament, is named for its 13-ton bell, Ben. (📖 For more on Big Ben, see page 15.) Tourists can enter the Houses of Parliament when Parliament is in session to see the impressive interior and view debates in either the bickering House of Commons or the genteel House of Lords. Otherwise, you must visit via a tour (either guided or audioguide).

 The Houses of Parliament have been the center of political power in England for nearly a thousand years—first as a royal residence (1042-1547), then as home to the increasingly powerful Parliament. In 1834, a horrendous fire gutted the palace. It was rebuilt in a Neo-Gothic style of pointed arches, stained-glass windows, spires, and saint-like statues. Today, "Westminster" (as Brits call the place) appears almost nightly on TV, as the impressive backdrop to the latest political news.

 **Westminster Hall**—covering 16,000 square feet—survived the 1834 fire, and is one of the oldest (from 1097) and most important structures in England. Its self-supporting oak-timber "hammer-beam" roof uses a complex system of curved braces and arches that distribute the weight of the roof outward, so there's no need for supporting pillars. It was in this historic hall that the king once presided on his throne, where England's vaunted legal system was developed, and where King Charles I was sentenced to death. In more recent times, the hall has hosted the lying-in-state of the Queen Mother and a speech by then-president Barack Obama.

SIGHTS

The Houses of Parliament's vast Westminster Hall, with its ingenious wooden roof

**St. Stephen's Hall** is where visitors wait to enter the House of Commons. This long, beautifully lit room was the original House of Commons for three centuries (from 1550 until the fire of 1834). After the fire, the hall was rebuilt. The stained-glass windows—forming a tall, rectangular grid—are a textbook example of the "Perpendicular" Gothic style used by architect Charles Barry. Next, you reach the **Central Lobby,** where visitors wait to visit the House of Lords (this is where the term "lobbying" comes from). This octagonal, high-vaulted room is often called the "heart of British government," because it sits in the geographical center of the sprawling, 1,100-room palace.

The **Lords Chamber** (which you view from an upper-level gallery) is church-like and impressive, with stained glass, intricately carved walls, and red-upholstered benches. At the far end is the Queen's gilded throne. The House of Lords consists of about 800 members, who are not elected by popular vote. Some are nobles who've inherited the position, others are appointed by the Queen. These days, their role is advisory; they have no real power to pass laws on their own.

The **Commons Chamber** is much less grandiose, but this is where the sausage gets made. The House of Commons is as power-ful as the Lords, prime minister, and Queen combined. Some 650-plus

Members of Parliament assemble on the green-upholstered benches to debate and pass laws. The ruling party is to the left, and the opposition to the right, with the canopied Speaker's Chair in between. The table in the center has two wooden chests that serve as lecterns, one for each side. The Chamber is at its liveliest when the prime minister visits (usually on Wed) to stand at the lectern and defend his policies, while the opposition grumbles and harrumphs in displeasure.

▶ *Free when Parliament is in session—generally Oct-late July, House of Commons—Mon 14:30-22:30, Tue-Wed 11:30-19:30, Thu 9:30-17:30; House of Lords—Mon-Tue 14:30-22:00, Wed 15:00-22:00, Thu 11:00-19:30; last entry depends on debates; exact schedule at www.parliament.uk. During recess (late July-Sept) and Sat year-round you must visit with a paid tour: audioguide-£19.50, guided tour-£26.50, 1.5 hours. Confirm schedule and reserve at www.parliament.uk or by calling 020/7219-4114; same-day tickets can sell out (ticket office open Mon-Fri 10:00-16:00, Sat 9:00-16:30, closed Sun, in Portcullis House next to Westminster Tube Station, entrance on Victoria Embankment). For tours, arrive at the visitors entrance on Cromwell Green 20 minutes before your tour time to clear security.*

*Crowd-Beating Tips: For the public galleries, lines tend to be longest at the start of each session, particularly on Wednesdays; the later in the day you enter, the less crowded (and less exciting) it is.*

## ▲▲▲Churchill War Rooms

In the darkest days of World War II—with Nazi bombs raining down on a helpless London and invasion imminent—Britain's government hunkered down in this underground headquarters to direct the war effort. It was here that Prime Minister Winston Churchill lived, worked, and made stirring radio speeches that inspired Brits to carry on.

Today you can tour the well-preserved, 27-room, heavily fortified nerve center of the war effort from 1939 to 1945. See Churchill's room, the map room, and other offices, while listening to recordings of first-person accounts. You'll see how British gentility survived even as the city was bombarded.

The Churchill Museum dissects every aspect of the man behind the famous cigar, bowler hat, and V-for-victory sign. You get a taste of Winston's wit, irascibility, work ethic, passion for painting, American connections, writing talents, and drinking habits. It traces the varied stages of his long life (1874-1965): newspaper reporter, war hero,

Churchill War Rooms—a WWII underground HQ   Banqueting House—colorful Rubens ceiling

Conservative politician, Liberal politician, and author. In the 1930s, he was a political pariah for ranting about the growing threat of Hitler's fascism. When his vision proved right, he was appointed prime minister on the day Hitler invaded the Netherlands. After the war, it was Churchill who warned of the Soviet threat, coining the phrase "Iron Curtain." Touring this place, you have to wonder how different the world might have been today without Winston Churchill. Allow 1-2 hours for your visit.

▶ *£22 for timed-entry ticket (buy online in advance to avoid long ticket-buying lines and ensure entry), includes essential audioguide, daily 9:30-18:00, July-Aug until 19:00, last entry one hour before closing; on King Charles Street, 200 yards off Whitehall—follow signs, Tube: Westminster; tel. 020/7930-6961, www.iwm.org.uk/churchill-war-rooms.*

## ▲Banqueting House

England's first Renaissance building (1619-1622) has an impressive great hall topped with ceiling paintings by Peter Paul Rubens. Built as the dining hall and de facto throne room for King James I, it symbolized his "divine right" management style—the belief that God had anointed him to rule. The hall is the only highlight of the visit—at 55 feet wide, 55 feet high, and 110 feet long, it's a perfect double cube. The large, colorful ceiling paintings (up to 28 feet by 20 feet) portray James I as king of the whole world, crowned by Greek gods who bless him. The Banqueting House's most famous role was as the place where James' son, Charles I, was executed—and divine-right rule ended.

▶ *£7, includes audioguide, daily 10:00-17:00, may close for government functions—though it's always open at least until 13:00 (call ahead* *for recorded info), located along Whitehall, Tube: Westminster, tel. 020/3166-6155, www.hrp.org.uk.*

    📖 For more on the exterior, see page 22 in the Westminster Walk chapter.

## On Trafalgar Square

### ▲▲Trafalgar Square

London's central square, the climax of most marches and demonstrations, is arguably the center of the vast city.

    📖 See page 24 in the Westminster Walk chapter.

### ▲▲▲National Gallery

Britain's top collection of paintings is also one of the world's greatest collections—a microcosm of European art history, from medieval to Michelangelo to Monet and Van Gogh.

    📖 See the National Gallery Tour chapter.

### ▲▲National Portrait Gallery

Rock groupies, book lovers, movie fans, gossipmongers, and even historians all can find at least one favorite celebrity here. From Elizabeth I to Elizabeth II, Byron to Bowie, and Brontës to Beatles, the National Portrait Gallery is a Who's Who of 500 years of Britain's most fascinating people.

    Some highlights: Henry VIII and wives, portraits of the "Virgin Queen" Elizabeth I, the only real-life portrait of William Shakespeare, Charles I with his head on, Queen Victoria and her era, and the present royal family.

    The collection is well-described, not huge, and in historical sequence, from the 16th century on the second floor to today's royal family, usually housed on the ground floor.

▶ *Free, £5 suggested donation, special exhibits extra; daily 10:00-18:00, Fri until 21:00; excellent audioguide-£3, entry 100 yards off Trafalgar Square, Tube: Charing Cross or Leicester Square, tel. 020/7306-0055, www.npg.org.uk.*

### ▲St. Martin-in-the-Fields

The church, built in the 1720s with a Gothic spire atop a Greek-type temple, is an oasis of peace on busy Trafalgar Square. Though the interior is so-so, the venue is renowned for its concerts. Consider a lunchtime concert (£3.50 suggested donation; Mon, Tue, and Fri at 13:00), an evening concert (£9-29, several nights a week at 19:30), or Wednesday night jazz (£8-15, at 20:00). See the website for the full schedule. The church basement has a concert ticket office, gift shop, brass-rubbing center, and the recommended Café in the Crypt.

▶ *Free, donations welcome; Mon-Fri 8:30-18:00, Sat-Sun from 9:00, closed to visitors during services; Tube: Charing Cross, tel. 020/7766-1100, www.stmartin-in-the-fields.org.*

## The West End and Nearby

Once located "west" of the medieval walled city of London, this area is now London's liveliest. Theaters, pubs, restaurants, shopping, museums, and nightlife abound. ▲**Leicester Square** and ▲**Piccadilly Circus** form the nucleus of this area. To the north lie London's Chinatown, the theaters of Shaftesbury Avenue, and the trendy ▲**Soho** neighborhood. ▲▲**Covent Garden**—an arcade bristling with shops and colorful street life—is nearby, as are the shops of Regent Street. The best Tube stops are Leicester Square and Piccadilly.

📖 For more on all of the above sights, see the West End Walk chapter.

### ▲London Transport Museum

This modern, well-presented museum, located right at Covent Garden, is fun for kids and thought-provoking for adults (if a bit overpriced). The growth of Europe's third-biggest city has been made possible by its public transit system.

Take the elevator to the top floor...and the year 1800, when horse-drawn vehicles ruled the road. London invented the notion of a public bus traveling a set route that anyone could board without a reservation. The first floor explores the world's first underground Metro system, which used steam-powered locomotives. On the ground floor, horses and trains are replaced by cars, taxis, double-decker buses, streetcars, and 20th-century congestion. Learn how city planners hope to improve efficiency and transit coverage, and explore an exhibit that lets you imagine futuristic modes of transportation.

▶ *£18, daily 10:00-18:00, last entry 45 minutes before closing; pleasant café with Covent Garden view; Tube: Covent Garden, tel. 020/7379-6344, www.ltmuseum.co.uk.*

SIGHTS

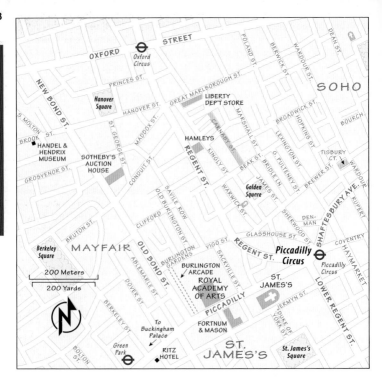

▲Courtauld Gallery

This gallery, part of the Courtauld Institute of Art, may be closed for a multiyear renovation when you visit. If it is open, you'll see medieval European paintings and works by Rubens, the Impressionists (Manet, Monet, and Degas), Post-Impressionists (Cézanne and an intense Van Gogh self-portrait), and more. The gallery is located within the grand Somerset House; enjoy the riverside eateries and the courtyard featuring a playful fountain.

▶ £7, price can change with exhibit; generally daily 10:00-18:00 but may be closed for renovation; in Somerset House on the Strand, Tube: Temple or Covent Garden, recorded info tel. 020/7848-2526, www.courtauld.ac.uk.

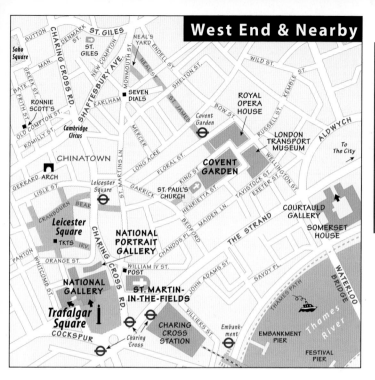

## Buckingham Palace

The working headquarters of the British monarchy, Buckingham Palace is where the Queen carries out her official duties as the head of state. She and other members of the royal family also maintain apartments here. The property hasn't always been this grand—James I (1603-1625) first brought the site under royal protection as a place for his mulberry plantation, for rearing silkworms. The wide boulevard called The Mall was built in 1911 as a ceremonial approach.

For tourists, there are several sights to see: the palace State Rooms (only open in summer), the Queen's Gallery art collection in a palace annex, and the stables of the adjoining Royal Mews (if seeing more than one of these sights, combo-tickets are available—check at

Buckingham Palace—the Queen's humble home    Changing of the Guard—maximum pageantry

the ticket desk). But most tourists are more interested in the Changing of the Guard, which is free to view (Tube: Victoria, St. James's Park, or Green Park, or hop into a black cab and say, "Buck House, please"; tel. 0303/123-7301—but Her Majesty rarely answers, www.royalcollection.org.uk).

▲**State Rooms:** This lavish home has been Britain's royal residence since 1837, when the newly ascended Queen Victoria moved in. When today's Queen is at home, the royal standard flies (a red, yellow, and blue flag); otherwise, the Union Jack flaps in the wind. The Queen opens her palace to the public—but only for a couple of months in summer, when she's out of town.

▶ *£25 for State Rooms and throne room, includes audioguide; late July-Sept only, daily 9:30-19:30, Sept until 18:30, last entry 75 minutes before closing; limited to 8,000 visitors a day by timed entry; come early to the palace's Visitor Entrance (opens at 9:00), or book ahead in person, by phone, or online.*

**Queen's Gallery at Buckingham Palace:** A small sampling of Queen Elizabeth's personal collection of art is on display in five rooms in a wing adjoining the palace. The exhibits change two or three times a year and are lovingly described by the included audioguide. Because the gallery is small and security is tight (involving lines), visit this gallery only if you're a patient art lover. Men shouldn't miss the mahogany-trimmed urinals.

▶ *£12 but can change depending on exhibit, daily 10:00-17:30, from 9:30 late July-Sept, last entry 75 minutes before closing.*

**Royal Mews:** These are the Queen's working stables, best seen with the included audioguide or hourly guided tour (April-Oct only,

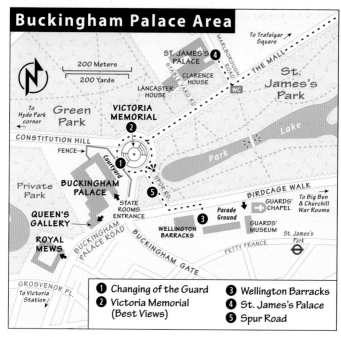

# Buckingham Palace Area

**To Trafalgar Square**

ST. JAMES'S ❹ PALACE

THE MALL

St. James's Park

200 Meters
200 Yards

CLARENCE HOUSE

LANCASTER HOUSE

**To Hyde Park corner**

Green Park

**VICTORIA MEMORIAL** ❷

WC

Lake

CONSTITUTION HILL

Park

FENCE

Courtyard ❶

**BUCKINGHAM PALACE**

Private Park

❺

SPUR RD

BIRDCAGE WALK

GUARDS' CHAPEL

**To Big Ben & Churchill War Rooms**

STATE ROOMS ENTRANCE

**QUEEN'S GALLERY**

Parade Ground ❸

GUARDS' MUSEUM

St. James's Park

**ROYAL MEWS**

WELLINGTON BARRACKS

PETTY FRANCE

BUCKINGHAM PALACE ROAD

BUCKINGHAM GATE

GROSVENOR PL.
**To Victoria Station**

❶ Changing of the Guard
❷ Victoria Memorial (Best Views)
❸ Wellington Barracks
❹ St. James's Palace
❺ Spur Road

STABLE YARD RD.

MARLBOROUGH ROAD

SIGHTS

45 minutes). You'll see only a few of the Queen's 30 horses, a fancy car, and a bunch of old carriages.

▶ £12, daily 10:00-17:00, off-season until 16:00, closed Sun in Nov and all of Dec-Jan; last entry 45 minutes before closing.

## ▲▲Changing of the Guard at Buckingham Palace

This is the spectacle every London visitor has to see at least once: stone-faced, bearskin-hatted guards changing posts with much fanfare, accompanied by a brass band.

The main attraction is the half-hour ceremony that takes place in the forecourt (between the palace and the fence) in front of Buckingham Palace. At 11:00 a batch of fresh guards meets the Old Guard in the courtyard, where the captain of the Old Guard hands over the keys.

If the actual changing of the Buckingham Palace guards is a must-see, show up at least an hour early to get a place front and center, next to the **fence** (shorter travelers should aim for two hours ahead in high season).

If you can't get a spot right by the gates, try the high ground on the circular **Victoria Memorial,** which can give you good (if more distant) views of the palace as well as the arriving and departing processions along The Mall and Spur Road.

If the main ceremony doesn't seem worth all the waiting and jostling, you can plant yourself on the route of a **string of processions** that happen before, during, and after the official guard changing at Buckingham Palace.

Show up at St. James's Palace by 10:30 to see its soon-to-be-off-duty guards mobilizing in the courtyard (grab a spot just across Marlborough Road from the courtyard). Just before they prepare to leave (at 10:43), march ahead of them down Marlborough Road to The Mall and pause at the corner to watch them parade past. Then cut through the park and head to the Wellington Barracks, where a fresh batch of guards is undergoing inspection before they leave (at 10:57) for Buckingham Palace. March along with them to the palace.

If the palace area is packed, make your way back up The Mall, to where it meets Stable Yard Road, in time to watch several more processions: relief guards coming from the palace to Clarence House (11:10); more guards heading *toward* Buckingham Palace (11:25); and cavalry guards en route from the Horse Guards to their barracks in Green Park (11:37).

Finally, at about 11:45, plant yourself back at the corner of The Mall and Marlborough Road for a great photo op as one last procession, the bulk of St. James's Palace New Guard, makes its way from Buckingham Palace to start its shift.

▸ *Free, May-July daily at 11:00, Aug-April Sun-Mon, Wed, and Fri, no ceremony in very wet weather; exact schedule subject to change—call 020/7766-7300 for the day's plan, or check www.householddivision. org.uk (search "Changing the Guard").*

# A Page of History

**The Beginnings:** In 55 BC, Julius Caesar invaded, and "Londinium" became a river-trade town and the hub of Britain. As Rome fell (AD 410), London was attacked by Saxons and Vikings. In 1066 the Normans invaded and built the Tower of London. As the city grew—London Bridge, Old St. Paul's—it became clear to wannabe kings that whoever controlled London controlled Britain. Monarchs built their palaces west of the city walls, near Westminster Abbey.

**1500s:** Charismatic Henry VIII thrust England onto the world stage, and London's population swelled to 50,000. His daughter, Elizabeth I, reigned over a cultural renaissance of sea exploration, scientific discovery, literature (Shakespeare), and fine manners.

**1600s:** Just when things were going so well, the Great Plague (1665) and Great Fire (1666) devastated the wooden city. London rebuilt—Christopher Wren designed St. Paul's and dozens of other churches—but the center of gravity had shifted to the West End.

**1700s:** Britannia ruled the waves, and London (pop. 500,000) bloomed with Georgian architecture, theater, daily newspapers, and the sounds of Handel's *Messiah*. When Admiral Nelson defeated Napoleon at sea, and the Duke of Wellington finished him off at Waterloo, Britain emerged as the world's No. 1 power.

**1800s:** Britain under Queen Victoria reigned supreme, steaming into the modern age with railroads, factories, telephones, and the first Underground. Meanwhile, Charles Dickens chronicled the darker elements, and Jack the Ripper prowled the soot-stained tenements.

**20th Century:** Two world wars whittled Britain down from an empire to a struggling nation. During World War II, the Nazi "Blitz" bombing campaign leveled eastern London. Britain's colonies demanded independence, and London was flooded with immigrants. In the 1960s, "Swinging London" was a center for rock music (The Beatles, The Stones, The Who), fashion, and joie de vivre. The 1970s brought massive unemployment. The 1980s brought a conservative reaction and worldwide attention on Princess Diana.

**21st Century:** London is again one of the world's greatest cities, a hub of banking, art, technology, pop music, TV, and film.

# NORTH LONDON

### ▲▲▲British Museum

As home to artifacts through the ages, a visit here is like taking a long hike through *Encyclopedia Britannica* National Park.

See the 📖 British Museum Tour chapter or download my free 🎧 audio tour.

### ▲Sir John Soane's Museum

Architects and fans of eclectic knickknacks love this quirky place, as do fans of interior decor. Tour this furnished townhouse on a bird-chirping square and see 19th-century chairs, lamps, and carpets, wood-paneled nooks and crannies, stained-glass skylights, and Soane's collection of ancient relics and curios. His famous paintings include Hogarth's series on *The Rake's Progress* (read the fun plot) and several excellent Canalettos. In 1833, just before his death, Soane established his house as a museum, stipulating that it be kept in the state he left it. You'll leave wishing you'd known the man.

▶ *Free, donations appreciated; Wed-Sun 10:00-17:00, closed Mon-Tue; often long entry lines (especially Sat), knowledgeable volunteers in most rooms, guidebook-£5; free 30-minute tour of private apartment at 13:15 and 14:00, £15 one-hour highlights tour must be booked ahead online and runs Thu-Sun at 12:00 plus Sat-Sun at 11:00; 13 Lincoln's Inn Fields, quarter-mile southeast of British Museum, Tube: Holborn, tel. 020/7405-2107, www.soane.org.*

### ▲▲▲British Library

A manageable collection of the literary treasures of Western

Wallace Collection—aristocratic art

Madame Tussauds—Fab Four and more, in wax

civilization, from early Bibles to the Magna Carta to Shakespeare's *Hamlet* to Beatles lyrics.

See the 📖 British Library Tour chapter or download my free 🎧 audio tour.

## ▲Wallace Collection

Sir Richard Wallace's fine collection of 17th-century Dutch Masters, 18th-century French Rococo, medieval armor, and aristocratic fancies fills a sumptuous mansion. Paintings include *The Laughing Cavalier* by Frans Hals (as you walk by, his smirking eyes follow you) and *The Swing* by Jean-Honoré Fragonard (featuring an oblivious husband, a lurking lover, and a swinging wife).

▶ *Free, £5 suggested donation, daily 10:00-17:00, audioguide-£4, free "highlights" tours daily at 14:30, Fri-Sun also at 11:30; Tube: Bond Street, tel. 020/7563-9500, www.wallacecollection.org.*

## Sights that Stay Open Late

Most sightseeing in London winds down by 18:00, but there are several exceptions. Keep in mind that many of these sights stop admitting visitors well before their posted closing times.

**Madame Tussauds:** July-Aug daily until 18:00 (last entry time; stays open about 2 hours later)

**Westminster Abbey** (main church only): Wed until 19:00

**British Library:** Mon-Thu until 20:00

**London Eye:** Last ascent daily 20:30 or later in summer, until 18:00 Sept-May

**British Museum** (some galleries): Fri until 20:30

**National Gallery:** Fri until 21:00

**National Portrait Gallery:** Fri until 21:00

**Houses of Parliament:** House of Commons—Oct-late July Mon until 22:30, Tue-Wed until 19:30; House of Lords—Oct-late July Mon-Wed until 22:00, Thu until 19:30

**Tate Modern:** Fri-Sat until 22:00

**Victoria and Albert Museum** (some galleries): Fri until 22:00

▲Madame Tussauds Waxworks

This waxtravaganza is gimmicky, crass, and crazy expensive, but dang fun...a hit with the kind of tourists who skip the British Museum. The original Madame Tussaud did wax casts of heads lopped off during the French Revolution (such as Marie-Antoinette's). She took her show on the road and ended up in London in 1835. These days, the place is one giant, crowded, chaotic photo-op, with everyone jockeying for position to pose next to some famous dummy. They're eerily realistic. Count how many times you say "excuse me" after bumping into a wax figure.

Besides the lineup of A-list stars, you'll see sports heroes (including some unfamiliar-to-Americans cricket players and footballers), the royal family (pose with the Queen, Will, and Kate...or settle for

## Beatles Sights

London's city center is surprisingly devoid of sights associated with the famous '60s rock band. For a photo op, go to **Abbey Road** and walk the famous crosswalk pictured on the *Abbey Road* album cover (northwest of Regent's Park, Tube: St. John's Wood, memorabilia at the small kiosk in station). From the Tube station, it's a five-minute walk west down Grove End Road to the intersection with Abbey Road. The Abbey Road recording studio is the low-key white building to the right of Abbey House (it's still a working studio, so you can't go inside). To re-create the famous cover photo, shoot the crosswalk from the roundabout as you face north up Abbey Road. Shoes are optional.

Nearby is **Paul McCartney's current home** (7 Cavendish Avenue): Continue down Grove End Road, turn left on Circus Road, and then right on Cavendish. Please be discreet.

The **Beatles Store** is at 231 Baker Street (Tube: Baker Street). It's small—some Beatles-logo T-shirts, mugs, pins, and old vinyl (open eight days a week, 10:00-18:30, tel. 020/7935-4464, www.beatlesstorelondon.co.uk; another rock memorabilia store is across the street).

Charles and Camilla), scientists, artists, writers, musicians, and world leaders.

▸ *£35, up to 25 percent cheaper online, combo-deal with London Eye and other attractions; varying hours (check online), but roughly July-Aug and school holidays daily 8:30-18:00, Sept-June Mon-Fri 10:00-16:00, Sat-Sun 9:00-17:00, these are last entry times—it stays open roughly two hours later; Marylebone Road, Tube: Baker Street, tel. 0871-894-3000, www.madametussauds.com.*

*To avoid the ticket line, book a Priority Entrance ticket at least a day in advance. The place is less crowded after 15:00.*

# THE CITY

When Londoners say "The City," they mean the one-square-mile business center in East London that 2,000 years ago was Roman Londinium. The outline of the Roman city walls can still be seen in the arc of roads from Blackfriars Bridge to Tower Bridge. Within The

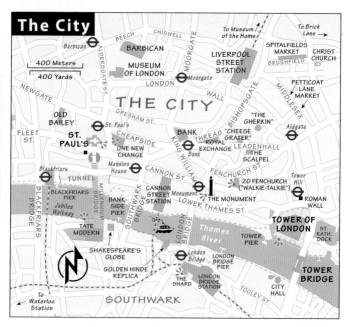

# The City

City are 23 churches designed by Sir Christopher Wren, mostly just ornamentation around St. Paul's Cathedral. Today, while home to only 10,000 residents, The City thrives with around 400,000 office workers coming and going daily. It's a fascinating district to wander on weekdays, but since almost nobody actually lives there, it's dull in the evening and on Saturday and Sunday.

## ▲▲▲St. Paul's Cathedral

There's been a church here since 604. When Old St. Paul's Cathedral was incinerated in the Great Fire of 1666, Sir Christopher Wren (1632-1723) was hired to build a new and bigger church on the spot. Even now, as skyscrapers encroach, Wren's 365-foot-high dome rises majestically above the rooftops of the neighborhood. St. Paul's is England's national church, and was the symbol of the city's survival of the Blitz of 1940. During "the Blitz"—when Nazi warplanes pummeled a defenseless London—St. Paul's was hit with 28 bombs. The surrounding neighborhood was absolutely flattened, but the church rose above it, seemingly miraculously, giving hope to London in its darkest hour. Today, St. Paul's is the nucleus of the Anglican faith, a living war memorial, and the final resting place of many great Londoners. You can climb the dome for expansive views.

The spacious nave, at 515 feet long and 250 feet wide, is Europe's fourth largest. Stroll up the nave—the same one Prince Charles and Lady Diana walked on their 1981 wedding day. When you reach the base of the soaring, 65,000-ton dome, stand and gasp upward. The dome you see is only the innermost of Wren's ingenious three-in-one design. The second dome is visible when you look up through the opening at the top to see the light-filled lantern. Finally, the whole thing is covered on the outside by a third and final dome—the shell of lead-covered wood that you see from the street.

Wren's creation has the clean lines and geometric simplicity of the age of Newton, when reason was holy and God set the planets spinning in perfect geometrical motion. For more than 40 years, Wren worked on this site, overseeing every detail. At age 75, he got to look up and see his son place a cross on top of the dome, completing the masterpiece. On the floor directly beneath the dome is a brass grate with Wren's name and epitaph: *Lector, si monumentum requiris circumspice*—"Reader, if you seek his monument, look around you."

In the north transept, find the big painting *The Light of the World* (1904), by William Holman Hunt. In the dark of night, Jesus—with a lantern, halo, jeweled cape, and crown of thorns—approaches an out-of-the-way home in the woods, knocks on the door, and listens for an invitation to come in. The painting is one of the world's best known, but critics have always savaged it, and it was once listed as number seven on a list of "Britain's Ten Worst Paintings."

Approaching the altar, you'll pass the abstract statue *Mother and Child* by Britain's greatest modern sculptor, Henry Moore, who was inspired by the sight of British moms nursing babies in WWII bomb shelters. Behind the altar is the American Memorial Chapel. The 500-page Roll of Honor lists the 28,000 Yanks based in Britain who sacrificed their lives to save Britain during World War II. The stained-glass windows even feature American iconography amid the saints. Spot the American eagle (center window, to the left of Christ), George

St. Paul's, with Wren's 365-foot dome

Nelson lies directly beneath the dome.

Washington (right window, upper-right corner), and symbols of all 50 states.

Continuing on, you'll pass a shrouded statue of John Donne, the well-known poet ("No man is an island..."), who was also a passionate preacher in old St. Paul's (1621-1631).

To climb the dome, it's 528 steps to the top—no elevator. The tower has three levels, called galleries. The climb gets steeper, narrower, and more claustrophobic as you go higher. You don't have to do all three levels, but once you start to the next level, you can't turn back. After the initial 257 steps, you first reach the Whispering Gallery, with nice views of the church interior. The dome is constructed with such acoustic precision that sweet nothings whispered from one side of the dome can (supposedly) be heard on the opposite side, 170 feet away. After another set of stairs, you're at the Stone Gallery, offering expansive outdoor views of London. Finally, a long, tight staircase takes you to the top of the cupola, the Golden Gallery, with stunning views of the entire city.

You can also descend to the church crypt, where many famous people are buried (use the free church map to locate them), including Horatio Nelson (who wore down Napoleon) and the Duke of Wellington (who finished Napoleon off). The tomb of Christopher Wren—the man who built this glorious cathedral—is buried off in a corner in a humble grave marked with just a plain black slab.

▶ *£20, cheaper online, includes church entry, dome climb, crypt, tour, and audioguide; Mon-Sat 8:30-16:30 (dome opens at 9:30), closed Sun except for worship; book ahead online to skip the line, guided tours offered; Tube: St. Paul's, tel. 020/7246-8350, www.stpauls.co.uk.*

**Music:** Evensong services are free (Mon-Sat at 17:00, Sun at 15:15;

# Harry Potter's London

Harry Potter's story is set in a magical Britain, and the places mentioned in the books are fictional, but you can visit many real (if un-magical) film locations.

Harry first realizes his wizard powers when talking with a boa constrictor, filmed at the **London Zoo's Reptile House** in Regent's Park (Tube: Great Portland Street). **Big Ben** and **Parliament,** along the Thames, welcome Harry to the modern city inhabited by non-magical Muggles. Harry shops with Hagrid in glass-roofed **Leadenhall Market** (Tube: Bank) along Bull's Head Passage. Goblin-run Gringotts Wizarding Bank was filmed in the chandeliered entryway of **Australia House** (Tube: Temple).

Harry catches the train to Hogwarts at **King's Cross/St. Pancras Station,** departing from magical **platform 9¾** (where the station has placed a sign and disappearing luggage cart near real platform 9—and a Harry Potter gift shop). In the *Prisoner of Azkaban* film, Harry careens through the city on a three-decker bus that dumps him off at the southeast edge of **Borough Market** (Tube: London Bridge). In the *Half-Blood Prince* film, the **Millennium Bridge** collapses into the Thames. For the *Deathly Hallows* films, the real government offices of **Whitehall** serve as the location for the Ministry of Magic.

Other London settings, like Diagon Alley, only exist at **Leavesden Film Studios** (20 miles north of London), where most of the films' interiors were shot. Here, Harry Potter pilgrims can see many of the original sets and props on the Warner Bros. Studio Tour (£45, purchase timed-entry ticket online in advance, tel. 0345-084-0900, www.wbstudiotour.co.uk). Visiting Leavesden takes most of a day. You can get there via a train-and-shuttle bus combination from Euston Station or via a pricey-but-convenient Golden Tours bus from near Victoria Station (www.goldentours.com).

Mon evensong occasionally spoken, not sung); nonpaying visitors are not allowed to linger afterward.

🎧 Download my free St. Paul's Cathedral audio tour.

## ▲Old Bailey

To view the British legal system in action—lawyers in little blond wigs speaking legalese with an upper-crust accent—spend a few minutes in the visitors' gallery at the Old Bailey courthouse, called the "Central Criminal Court." Don't enter under the dome; continue up the block about halfway to the modern part of the building—the entry is at Warwick Passage.

▶ *Free, generally Mon-Fri 10:00-13:00 & 14:00-17:00, closed Sat-Sun; tight security—check bags at Capable Travel agency, just down the street at 4 Old Bailey (£5/bag); located on Old Bailey Street, follow signs to public entrance; Tube: St. Paul's, tel. 020/7248-3277, www. cityoflondon.gov.uk.*

## ▲Museum of London

This regular stop for local school kids gives the best overview of London history in town. Scale models and costumes help you visualize everyday life in the city through history—from Neanderthals, to Romans, to Elizabethans, to Victorians, to Mods, to today. The displays are chronological, spacious, and informative without being overwhelming, with enough whiz-bang multimedia displays (including the Plague and the Great Fire) to spice up otherwise humdrum artifacts.

▶ *Free, daily 10:00-18:00, last entry one hour before closing, see the day's events board for special talks and tours; café, lockers, 150 London Wall at Aldersgate Street, Tube: Barbican or St. Paul's plus a 5-minute walk, tel. 020/7001-9844, www.museumoflondon.org.uk.*

## ▲▲▲Tower of London

This vast castle complex stars the crown jewels, witty Beefeater tours, and the executioner's site that dispensed with a couple of Henry VIII's wives.

    📖 See the Tower of London Tour chapter.

## Tower Bridge

The iconic Tower Bridge—often mistakenly called London Bridge—was built in 1894 as a hydraulically powered drawbridge to accommodate the growing East End. You can tour the bridge and its workings at the Tower Bridge Exhibition.

▶ *£9.80, daily 10:00-18:00 in summer, 9:30-17:30 in winter, enter at northwest tower, Tube: Tower Hill, tel. 020/7403-3761, www.towerbridge. org.uk.*

# THE SOUTH BANK

South of the Thames is a thriving area tied together by a riverside pedestrian path called the Jubilee Walkway (worth ▲). Stretching from the London Eye to London Bridge, it offers grand views of the city skyline across the river. On a sunny day, this is the place to see London out strolling.

The area hosts major sights—Shakespeare's Globe, the Tate Modern—plus some tacky ones, all spiced with pleasant pubs, theaters, and cafés. Several Thames cruise boats stop along the South Bank (see page 160; Tube: Waterloo, Southwark, London Bridge).

## ▲▲London Eye

This giant Ferris wheel, towering above London opposite Big Ben, is London's answer to the Eiffel Tower. Riding it is a memorable experience, even though London doesn't have much of a skyline, and the price is borderline outrageous.

Twenty-eight people ride in each of its 32 air-conditioned capsules (representing the boroughs of London) for the 30-minute rotation (you go around only once). From the top of this 443-foot-high wheel—the second-highest public viewpoint in the city—even Big Ben looks small. Built to celebrate the new millennium, the Eye has become a permanent fixture on the London skyline.

Your ticket also includes a bombastic-but-fun, four-minute, 3-D movie. By the Eye there's a cotton-candy tourist zone of kitschy, kid-friendly attractions, as well as Thames cruise boats.

▶ *£30, cheaper online, family ticket and combo-ticket with Madame Tussauds available; daily 10:00-20:30 or later, Sept-May generally 11:00-18:00, check website for latest schedule, Tube: Waterloo or Westminster.*
   ***Crowd-Beating Tips:*** *The Eye is busiest 11:00-17:00, especially on weekends and in summer. At these times, buy timed-entry tickets in advance at www.londoneye.com or at the box office. The Fast Track ticket may still entail a wait—it's not worth the expense.*

## ▲▲Imperial War Museum

This impressive, engrossing museum covers the conflicts of the 20th and 21st centuries with lots of artifacts and video clips. War wonks love the place, as do history buffs who enjoy patiently reading displays.

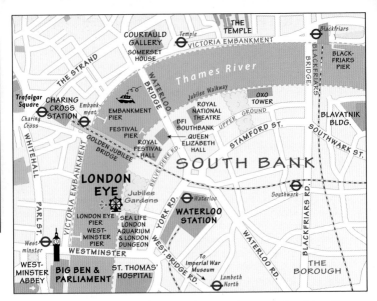

For the rest, there are enough interactive experiences and multimedia exhibits and submarines for the kids to climb in to keep it interesting.

Highlights include the WWI galleries and the WWII rooms. You'll see vintage planes, tanks, and a 50-foot V-2 rocket, the kind Hitler rained down on London. The Holocaust exhibit is one of the best on the subject anywhere. The displays continue through the Cold War, the Troubles in Northern Ireland, the wars in Iraq and Afghanistan, and terrorism. Rather than glorify war, the museum shines a light on the 100 million deaths of the 20th century—the tragic consequence of one of humankind's most persistent traits.

▶ Free, £5 suggested donation, special exhibits extra, daily 10:00-18:00, last entry one hour before closing, Tube: Lambeth North or Elephant and Castle; buses #3, #12, and #159 from Westminster area; tel. 020/7416-5000, www.iwm.org.uk.

## ▲▲Tate Modern

Dedicated in the spring of 2000, the striking museum fills a derelict

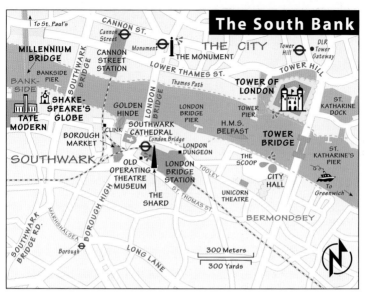

old power station across the river from St. Paul's—it opened the new century with art from the previous one. Its powerhouse collection includes Dalí, Picasso, Warhol, and much more. Of equal interest are the many temporary exhibits featuring more current, cutting-edge art. A new annex—built on the site of the power station's switch house and connected to the main building by skybridge—shows off more of the Tate's collection and has beautiful views from its 10th-floor terrace. Each year, the main hall features a different monumental installation by a prominent artist.

▶ *Free, £5 suggested donation, fee for special exhibits; open daily 10:00-18:00, Fri-Sat until 22:00, last entry to special exhibits 45 minutes before closing, especially crowded on weekend days (crowds thin out Fri and Sat evenings); free guided tours available, view restaurant on top floor, across the Millennium Bridge from St. Paul's; Tube: Southwark, London Bridge, St. Paul's, Mansion House, or Blackfriars; tel. 020/7887-8888, www.tate.org.uk.*

The high-caliber Imperial War Museum

Tate Modern—powerhouse art in a powerhouse

### ▲Millennium Bridge

The pedestrian bridge linking St. Paul's Cathedral and the Tate Modern opened in the year 2000. Almost immediately, the $25 million "bridge to the next millennium" started wobbling dangerously. Now stabilized, it's won praise for Sir Norman Foster's sleek minimalist design—370 yards long, four yards wide, of stainless steel with teak planks.

### ▲▲Shakespeare's Globe

This replica of the original Globe Theatre was built, half-timbered and thatched, as it was in Shakespeare's time. (This is the first thatched roof constructed in London since they were outlawed after the Great Fire of 1666.) It serves as a working theater by night and offers tours by day. The original Globe opened in 1599, debuting Shakespeare's play *Julius Caesar*. The Globe originally accommodated 2,200 seated and another 1,000 standing. Today, slightly smaller and leaving space for reasonable aisles, the theater holds 800 seated and 600 groundlings.

The working theater hosts authentic performances of Shakespeare's plays with actors in period costumes, modern interpretations of his works, and some works by other playwrights.

The complex's smaller Sam Wanamaker Playhouse—an indoor, horseshoe-shaped Jacobean theater—allows the show to go on in the winter, when it's too cold for performances in the outdoor Globe. While the Globe mainly presents Shakespeare's works, the playhouse tends to focus on the works of his contemporaries.

For details on attending a performance in either space, drop by the box office (details on page 164). While the play's the thing, a tour is worthwhile, too—and a nice way to see the impressively reconstructed

Shakespeare's Globe hosts plays (in summer) and lets visitors tour the theater and museum.

space if you don't have the time or attention span to devote to a full-length performance.

▶ *Tours last 40 minutes and depart every half hour (£17, April-mid-Oct last tours depart Mon at 17:00, Tue-Sat at 12:30, Sun at 11:30; off-season last tours at 17:00; complex also has a box office and eateries, from fancy to takeout; Tube: Mansion House or London Bridge plus a 10-minute walk; tel. 020/7902-1400, www.shakespearesglobe.com).*

## ▲Southwark

The area between the Tate Modern and London Bridge is known as Southwark (SUTH-uck). In Shakespeare's day, this was the rowdy neighborhood where Londoners went for a night of theater, bear-and-dog fights, brothels, and rollicking pubs. Today it's been gentrified, and within a few blocks (near Tube: London Bridge), you'll find several interesting (and some tacky) sights.

**The Clink Prison Museum:** This was, until 1780, where law-abiding citizens threw Southwark troublemakers. Today, it's a low-tech, tacky torture museum filling grotty old rooms with papier-mâché gore.

▶ *Overpriced at £7.50; Mon-Fri 10:00-18:00, Sat-Sun until 19:30, open later in summer; 1 Clink Street, Tube: London Bridge, tel. 020/7403-0900, www.clink.co.uk.*

**Golden Hinde Replica:** As we all learned in school, "Sir Francis Drake circumcised the globe with a hundred-foot clipper." Or something like that... This is a full-size, working replica of that 16th-century warship in which Drake circumnavigated the globe (1577-1580), becoming history's most successful pirate.

▶ *£5, daily 10:00-18:00, off-season until 17:00, Tube: London Bridge, tel. 020/7403-0123, www.goldenhinde.co.uk.*

▲**Southwark Cathedral:** Highlights include a Shakespeare memorial (right wall), a chapel to university-founding John Harvard (left wall), and evensong services (Tue-Fri 17:30, Sun 15:00, and some Sat at 16:00).

▶ *Free, £1 map serves as photo permit, Mon-Fri 8:00-18:00, Sat-Sun from 8:30, Tube: London Bridge, tel. 020/7367-6700, www.cathedral. southwark.anglican.org.*

**Borough Market:** For over 800 years, there's been a produce market here. These days there are as many people taking photos as buying fruit, cheese, and beautiful breads, but it's still a fun carnival atmosphere with fantastic stall food. For maximum market and minimum crowds, join the locals on Thursdays (full market open Wed-Sat 10:00-17:00). Located next to Southwark Cathedral, Tube: London Bridge; www.boroughmarket.org.uk.

**London Bridge:** Built in 1972, this is the unimpressive fourth incarnation of the famed 2,000-year-old river crossing. Farther east is the egg-shaped City Hall building and an outdoor amphitheater called The Scoop, which hosts free summer entertainment.

## ▲Old Operating Theatre Museum and Herb Garret

Climb a tight and creaky staircase to find a garret used to dry medicinal herbs, crude Victorian surgical instruments, and a special look at anesthetics—ether, chloroform, or three pints of ale.

Then you stumble upon Britain's oldest operating theater—a semicircular room accommodating 150 spectators—where doctors sawed off limbs while med students observed. The wood still bears bloodstains. Nearly one in three patients died. There was a fine line between Victorian-era surgeons and Jack the Ripper.

▶ *£6.50, Tue-Sun 10:30-17:00, Mon from 14:00, 9a St. Thomas Street, Tube: London Bridge, tel. 020/7188-2679, oldoperatingtheatre.com.*

## The Shard

Rocketing dramatically 1,020 feet above the south end of the London Bridge, this is by far the tallest building in Western Europe...for now. Seventy floors up are observation decks with exceptional views (and ticket prices as high as the building itself).

▶ *£39—book online in advance, advance ticket includes free return ticket in case of bad weather, otherwise pay 25 percent more on-site; least crowded on weekday mornings; daily 10:00-22:00, shorter hours Oct-March; Tube: London Bridge—use London Bridge exit and follow signs, tel. 0844-499-7111, www.theviewfromtheshard.com.*

# WEST LONDON

### ▲▲Tate Britain

Tate Britain specializes in British painting from the 16th century through modern times. The museum has a good representation of William Blake's religious sketches, the Pre-Raphaelites' naturalistic and detailed art, Gainsborough's aristocratic ladies, and the best collection anywhere of J. M. W. Turner's swirling works.

▶ *Free, £4 suggested donation, fee for special exhibits; daily 10:00-18:00, last entry 45 minutes before closing; free tours generally daily; Tube: Pimlico, tel. 020/7887-8888, www.tate.org.uk.*

### ▲Apsley House (Wellington Museum)

Having beaten Napoleon at Waterloo, Arthur Wellesley, the First Duke of Wellington, was given a huge fortune, with which he purchased London's ultimate address, Number One London. His mansion offers a nice interior, a few world-class paintings, and a glimpse at the life of the great soldier and two-time prime minister. Those who know something about Wellington ahead of time will appreciate the place much more than those who don't, as there's scarce biographical background. The place is well described by the included audioguide, which has sound bites from the current Duke of Wellington (who still lives at Apsley).

▶ *£10.30, Wed-Sun 11:00-17:00, closed Mon-Tue, shorter hours Nov-March, open only Sat-Sun in Jan-March, Tube: Hyde Park Corner, tel. 020/7499-5676, www.english-heritage.org.uk.*

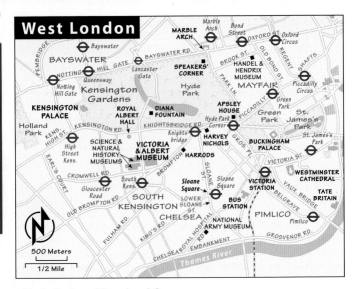

# West London

**▲Hyde Park and Speakers' Corner**

London's "Central Park," originally Henry VIII's hunting grounds, has more than 600 acres of lush greenery, Santander Cycles rental stations, the huge man-made Serpentine Lake (with rental boats and a lakeside swimming pool), the royal Kensington Palace (described next), and the ornate Neo-Gothic Albert Memorial across from the Royal Albert Hall (for more about the park, see www.royalparks.org.uk/parks/hyde-park). The western half of the park is known as Kensington Gardens.

On Sundays, from just after noon until early evening, **Speakers' Corner** offers soapbox oratory at its best (northeast corner of the park, Tube: Marble Arch). "The grass roots of democracy" is actually a holdover from when the gallows stood here and the criminal was allowed to say just about anything he wanted to before he swung. I dare you to raise your voice and gather a crowd—it's easy to do.

The **Princess Diana Memorial Fountain** honors the "People's Princess," who once lived in nearby Kensington Palace. The low-key circular stream is great for cooling off your feet on a hot day (Tube: Knightsbridge).

Tate Britain—art with deep British roots

Victoria and Albert—eclectic and surprising

## Kensington Palace

For nearly 150 years (1689-1837), Kensington was the royal residence, before Buckingham Palace became the official home of the monarch. Sitting primly on its pleasant parkside grounds, the palace gives a barren yet regal glimpse into royal life—particularly that of Queen Victoria, who was born and raised here.

After Queen Victoria moved the monarchy to Buckingham Palace, lesser royals bedded down at Kensington. Princess Diana lived here both during and after her marriage to Prince Charles (1981-1997). More recently, Will and Kate moved in. However, none of these more recent apartments are open to the public. The palace hosts a revolving series of temporary exhibits, some great, others not so. To see what's on during your visit, check online.

Outside the palace, garden enthusiasts enjoy the secluded Sunken Garden.

▶ *£17.50; daily 10:00-18:00, Nov-Feb until 16:00, last entry one hour before closing; a long 10-minute stroll through Kensington Gardens from either High Street Kensington or Queensway Tube stations, tel. 0844-482-7788, www.hrp.org.uk.*

## ▲▲▲Victoria and Albert Museum

The world's top collection of decorative arts (ceramics, stained glass, fine furniture, clothing, jewelry, carpets, and more) is an eclectic and surprisingly interesting assortment. Throw in historical artifacts, a few masterpieces of painting and sculpture, and a bed that sleeps seven, and you have a museum built for browsing.

Here's just a sample: five of Leonardo da Vinci's notebooks, underwear through the ages, a Chihuly chandelier, a life-size *David* with detachable fig leaf, Henry VIII's quill pen, and Mick Jagger's sequined jumpsuit. From the worlds of Islam and India, there are stunning carpets, the ring of the man who built the Taj Mahal, and a mechanical tiger that eats Brits. Best of all, the objects are all quite beautiful. You could spend days in the place. Pick up a museum map and wander at will.

▶ *Free, £5 donation requested, fee for some special exhibits, daily 10:00-17:45, some galleries open Fri until 22:00, free tours daily, on Cromwell Road in South Kensington, Tube: South Kensington, from the Tube station a long tunnel leads directly to museum, tel. 020/7942-2000, www.vam.ac.uk.*

## ▲▲Natural History Museum

Across the street from Victoria and Albert, this mammoth museum contains 50 million specimens of earth's treasures—living things in one half, inanimate rocks and geology in the other. In the main hall, above a big dinosaur skeleton and under a massive slice of sequoia tree, Charles Darwin sits as if upon a throne overseeing it all. Behind Darwin is the Cadogan Gallery, displaying the museum's greatest hits: a dodo skeleton, a moon rock, an extinct auk, etc.

Kids and non-science majors love the place. Well-explained and interactive exhibits cover dinosaurs, human evolution, creepy-crawlies, volcanoes, and more. Don't miss the meteorite from Mars and the Aurora Pyramid of Hope, displaying 296 diamonds showing their full range of natural colors. Pop into the wild collection of dinosaurs if only to hear English children exclaim, "Oh my goodness!"

▶ *Free, £5 donation requested, fee for special exhibits, daily 10:00-18:00, helpful £1 map, long tunnel leads directly from South Kensington Tube station to museum (follow signs), tel. 020/7942-5000, exhibit info and reservations tel. 020/7942-5011, www.nhm.ac.uk. Free visitor app available via the "Visit" section of the website.*

## ▲Science Museum

Next door to the Natural History Museum, this sprawling wonderland for curious minds is kid-perfect, with themes such as measuring time, exploring space, climate change, and the Information Age. It offers hands-on fun, with trendy technology exhibits, an IMAX theater (£11), a cool play area, and more.

▸ *Free, £5 donation requested, daily 10:00-18:00, last entry 45 minutes before closing, Exhibition Road, Tube: South Kensington, tel. 0333-241-4000, www.sciencemuseum.org.uk.*

# GREATER LONDON

London's excellent public transit makes a number of outlying sights accessible. I've highlighted a few of my favorites. Budget the better part of a sightseeing day to visit any of these. For Greenwich, Kew, and Hampton Court, consider a Thames boat cruise as a scenic alternative to the train or Tube (for more on cruises, see page 160).

## ▲▲Greenwich

Just downstream from London, Greenwich is the destination for all things salty, including the *Cutty Sark* clipper ship, the area's premier attraction (it's a good idea to reserve a ticket in advance and plan your day around your entry time). At the Royal Observatory, visitors pose for a photo-op along the prime meridian (0° longitude), straddling two hemispheres, while they set their watches to coordinate to Greenwich Mean Time, measured from here. Thanks to this time standard (and to seaworthy clocks that could be taken aboard ships), sailors could finally plot their east-west (longitudinal) location.

The National Maritime Museum holds everything from a giant working paddlewheel to the uniform Admiral Nelson wore when he was killed at Trafalgar (find the bullet hole). The town of Greenwich is a pleasant, manageable place for a riverside stroll, enjoying stunning Baroque architecture and open-air markets. Finish your stroll with lunch at the **$$ Trafalgar Tavern,** a pub Charles Dickens wrote about. Ahoy!

▸ *Most sights are open daily and many are free.*

*Getting There: Boats depart from the piers at Westminster, the London Eye, and the Tower of London (2/hour, 30-75 minutes). By train, catch the DLR from Bank-Monument Tube station to Cutty Sark (20 minutes, 5/hour, covered by any Tube pass).*

## ▲▲Kew Gardens

For a fine riverside park and a palatial greenhouse jungle to swing through, take the Tube or the boat to every botanist's favorite escape,

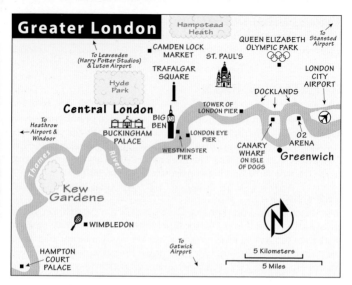

Kew Gardens. Wander across 300 acres among 50,000 different types of plants, representing the botanical diversity of our planet.

For a fragrant one-hour visit, concentrate on three buildings. The Palm House is a humid Victorian world of iron, glass, and tropical plants built in 1844. The Waterlily House has sights Monet would swim for. The Princess of Wales Conservatory is a modern greenhouse with many different climate zones growing countless cacti, bug-munching carnivorous plants, and more. The Xstrata Treetop Walkway, a 200-yard-long steel footbridge, puts you high in the canopy 60 feet above the ground. End your visit with a sun-dappled lunch or afternoon tea at the **$$ Orangery.**

▶ *£18, June-Aug £11 after 16:00; Mon-Thu 10:00-19:00, Fri-Sun until 20:00, closes earlier Sept-March, glasshouses close at 17:30 in high season—earlier off-season, free one-hour walking tours daily at 11:00 and 13:30, tel. 020/8332-5000, www.kew.org.*

***Getting There:*** *The Kew Gardens Tube station is two blocks from the main entrance. Boats run April-Oct from Westminster Pier.*

## ▲▲Hampton Court Palace

Fifteen miles up the Thames from downtown is the 500-year-old palace of Henry VIII. The stately Tudor palace overlooking the Thames was also home to Elizabeth I and Charles I. Visitors can see impressive Tudor rooms, including the King's apartments and a Great Hall with a magnificent hammer-beam ceiling. The industrial-strength Tudor kitchen kept 600 schmoozing courtiers thoroughly fed. The sculpted garden features a rare Tudor tennis court and a popular maze.

▸ *£23.70, cheaper online, family ticket available, includes audioguide; daily 10:00-18:00, Nov-March until 16:30, last entry one hour before closing—but you'll need 2-3 hours to see the place; café, tel. 0844-482-7777, www.hrp.org.uk.*

   ***Getting There:*** *Train (2/hour, 35 minutes) from London's Waterloo Station, or taxi (£20) from Kew Gardens. The 3- to 4-hour boat ride from Westminster Pier is relaxing and scenic.*

## ▲Windsor

Queen Elizabeth II's preferred residence is Windsor Castle, set in the compact, pedestrian-friendly town of Windsor (pop. 30,000). Here you can see a low-key Changing of the Guard, the castle's lavish staterooms (perhaps Britain's best), an impressive royal art collection, some royal tombs, and Queen Mary's dollhouse—a 1:12 scale palace in miniature.

▸ *£22.50, includes audioguide. To skip ticket lines, buy advance tickets online, daily 10:00-17:15, Nov-Feb until 16:15; St. George's Chapel closed Sun to tourists, last entry 75 minutes before closing, may close for special events—call first, tel. 020/7766-7324, www.rct.uk.*

   ***Getting There:*** *Trains run from both Paddington and Waterloo Stations (35-55 minutes, 2/hour).*

Kensington Palace—Will and Kate's home

Kew Gardens—tropical plants near London

# **Activities**

You'll never run out of things to do in London. This chapter offers suggestions for tours, shopping, and entertainment.

For an orientation tour, blow through the city on the open deck of a double-decker tour bus, take a pinch-me-I'm-in-London walk through a slice of the city with a chatty guide, or try a bike tour to lace together the best sights with a pleasant pedal through London's parks.

Whatever your taste or budget, London is great for shoppers. It's equally fun to gawk at ultra-posh high-end stores, and browse through colorful street markets. And there's no place like London for a theatrical performance, from Shakespeare to glitzy, fun musicals.

# TOURS

∩ To sightsee on your own, download my free Westminster Walk, British Museum, British Library, and St. Paul's Cathedral audio tours (see sidebar on page 10 for details).

## Hop-On, Hop-Off Double-Decker Bus Tours

**Original London Sightseeing** and **Big Bus London** both offer tours of the city's sightseeing highlights—an experience rated ▲▲▲. These once-over-lightly bus tours drive by all the famous sights, with at least one route with live guides and others with recorded narration (daily generally 8:30-20:00, until 17:00 in winter; Original—£32, RS%-up to four £6 discounts with this book, www.theoriginaltour.com; Big Bus—£37, cheaper online, www.bigbustours.com).

## London by Night Sightseeing Tour

Various companies offer a 1- to 2-hour circuit, but after hours, with no extras (e.g., walks, river cruises), at a lower price. **Golden Tours** buses depart from their offices on Buckingham Palace Road (£28, tel. 020/7630-2028; www.goldentours.com). **See London By Night** buses offer live English guides and daily departures from Green Park (£28.50, tel. 020/7183-4744, www.seelondonbynight.com).

## Driver-Guides

These guides have cars or a minibus and also do walking-only tours: **Janine Barton** (£390/half-day, £575/day, day tours outside of London start at £625 depending on the distance, registered Blue Badge guide, tel. 020/7402-4600, www.seeitinstyle.synthasite.com, jbsiis@aol.com); **Mike Dickson** (£345/half-day, £535/day, overnights also

Sample sights on a hop-on, hop-off bus tour.

Great local guides make sights come alive.

possible, registered Blue Badge guide; mobile 07769/905-811, michael. dickson5@btinternet.com); and **David Stubbs** (£375 for 1-3 people, £395 for 4-6 people, £415 for 7-8, mobile 07775-888-534, www. londoncountrytours.co.uk, info@londoncountrytours.co.uk).

## Walking Tours

Top-notch local guides lead (sometimes big) groups on walking tours—worth ▲▲—through specific slices of London's past. **London Walks** guides give top-quality two-hour walks (£12, cash only, walks offered year-round, private tours available, tel. 020/7624-3978, www. walks.com).

### Private Walks with Local Guides

Standard rates for London's registered Blue Badge guides are about £165-200 for four hours and £270 or more for nine hours (tel. 020/7611-2545, www.guidelondon.org.uk or www.britainsbestguides.org).

I know and like these fine local guides: **Sean Kelleher** (tel. 020/8673-1624, mobile 07764-612-770, sean@seanlondonguide.com); **Britt Lonsdale**, (£265/half-day, £365/day, tel. 020/7386-9907, mobile 07813-278-077, brittl@btinternet.com); **Joel Reid** (mobile 07887-955-720, joelyreid@gmail.com); **Tom Hooper** (mobile 07986-048-047, tomh1@btinternet.com); and **Gillian Chadwick** (£300/day, mobile 07889-976-598, gillychad@hotmail.co.uk). If you have a particular interest, London Walks (see earlier) has a huge selection of guides and can book one for your exact focus (£215/half-day).

## Bike Tours

**London Bicycle Tour Company** offers several tours leaving from their base next to the Imperial War Museum, south of the Thames (all are £27, see website for details). Sunday is the best, as there is less car traffic; optional helmets are included. They also rent bikes (£3.50/hour, £20/day; office open daily 9:30-18:00, shorter hours Nov-March, 74 Kennington Road, tel. 020/7928-6838, www.londonbicycle.com).

**Fat Tire Bike Tours** covers the highlights of downtown London, on two different itineraries (RS%-£2 discount with this book, mobile 078-8233-8779, www.fattiretours.com/london). They also offer a range of walking tours.

See London from a new vantage point on a sightseeing cruise.

### Cruise Boats

London offers many made-for-tourists cruises, most on slow-moving, open-top boats accompanied by entertaining commentary (an experience worth ▲▲). Several companies offer essentially the same trip. Generally speaking, you can either do a short city-center cruise by riding a boat 30 minutes from Westminster Pier to Tower Pier (handy for visiting the Tower of London), or take a longer cruise from Westminster to Greenwich (save time by taking the Tube back).

The three dominant companies are **City Cruises** (handy 45-minute cruise from Westminster Pier to Tower Pier; www.citycruises. com), **Thames River Services** (fewer stops, classic boats, friendlier and more old-fashioned feel; www.thamesriverservices.co.uk), and **Circular Cruise** (full cruise takes about an hour, operated by Crown River Services, www.circularcruise.london). The speedy **Thames Clippers** are designed more for no-nonsense transport than lazy sightseeing (www.thamesclippers.com). To compare your options in one spot, head to Westminster Pier.

## SHOPPING

London is famous for its shopping. The best and most convenient shopping streets are in the West End and West London (roughly between

Soho and Hyde Park). You'll find midrange shops along **Oxford Street** (running east from Tube: Marble Arch), and fancier shops along **Regent Street** (stretching south from Tube: Oxford Circus to Piccadilly Circus) and **Knightsbridge** (where you'll find Harrods and Harvey Nichols; Tube: Knightsbridge).

Most stores are open Monday through Saturday from roughly 9:00 or 10:00 until 17:00 or 18:00, with a late night on Wednesday or Thursday (usually until 19:00 or 20:00). Many close on Sundays. Large department stores stay open later during the week (until about 21:00 Mon-Sat) with shorter hours on Sundays.

## Fancy Department Stores

**Harrods** is London's most famous and touristy department store, with everything from elephants to toothbrushes (Brompton Road, Tube: Knightsbridge, tel. 020/7730-1234, www.harrods.com). **Harvey Nichols,** once Princess Diana's favorite, remains the department store *du jour* (109 Knightsbridge, Tube: Knightsbridge, tel. 020/7235-5000, www.harveynichols.com). **Fortnum & Mason** embodies old-fashioned, British upper-class taste (181 Piccadilly, Tube: Green Park, tel. 020/7734-8040, www.fortnumandmason.com). **Liberty** is known for its "Liberty Print" floral fabrics, well-stocked crafts department, and castle-like interior (Great Marlborough Street, Tube: Oxford Circus, tel. 020/7734-1234, www.liberty.co.uk).

## Street Markets

London's weekend flea markets are legendary, and there are early-morning produce markets any day of the week. Covent Garden's daily market is handy to other sightseeing (daily 10:30-18:00, tel. 020/7395-1350, www.coventgardenlondonuk.com).

Portobello Road Market is the classic London street market. Antiques, produce, garage-sale items, food stands, live music, and huge crowds create a festival atmosphere. On Saturdays, this funky-yet-quaint Notting Hill street of pastel-painted houses and offbeat antiques shops is enlivened even more with 2,000 additional stalls. On non-Saturdays, the street itself is fun to explore; I prefer Fridays—most stalls are open, with half the crowds of Saturday (Tube: Notting Hill Gate, tel. 020/7727-7684, www.portobelloroad.co.uk).

Camden Lock Market in north London is a huge, trendy arts-and-crafts festival. It runs daily 10:00-19:00, but is

Cruise to Camden Lock Market

Harrods—four acres of posh shopping

busiest on weekends (Tube: Camden Town, tel. 020/3763-9999, www.camdenmarket.com).

For a pleasant Sunday in the East End, take the Tube to Liverpool Street and visit the huge, covered Spitalfields Market (shops open daily until 17:00, www.spitalfields.co.uk). Then walk to the Petticoat Lane Market, where a line of stalls sits on the otherwise dull, glass-skyscraper-filled Middlesex Street; adjoining Wentworth Street is more characteristic (best on Sun, 9:00-14:00).

## VAT and Customs

**Getting a VAT Refund:** If you purchase more than £30 (about $40) worth of goods at a single store, you may be eligible to get a refund of the 20 percent Value-Added Tax (VAT). Get more details from your merchant or see www.ricksteves.com/vat.

**Customs for American Shoppers:** You can take home $800 worth of items per person duty-free, once every 31 days. You can bring in one liter of alcohol duty-free. For details on allowable goods, customs rules, and duty rates, visit http://help.cbp.gov.

# ENTERTAINMENT

London bubbles with top-notch entertainment seven days a week: plays, movies, concerts, exhibitions, walking tours, shopping, and children's activities. For the best list of what's happening and a look at the latest London scene, check www.timeout.com/london. The free monthly *London Planner* covers sights, events, and plays, though generally not as well as the Time Out website.

# Theater (a.k.a. "Theatre")

London's theater scene rivals Broadway's in quality and often beats it in price. Choose from 200 offerings—Shakespeare, musicals, comedies, thrillers, sex farces, cutting-edge fringe, revivals starring movie celebs, and more. London does it all well.

Nearly all big-name shows are hosted in the theaters of the West End, clustering around Soho (especially along Shaftesbury Avenue) between Piccadilly and Covent Garden. Well-known musicals may draw the biggest crowds, but the West End offers plenty of other crowd-pleasers, from revivals of classics to cutting-edge works by the hottest young playwrights.

**Buying Tickets:** It usually makes sense to simply buy tickets in London unless you have your heart set on a show that's likely to sell out. The famous TKTS Booth at Leicester Square sells discounted tickets (25-50 percent off) for many shows (£3/ticket service charge included, open Mon-Sat 10:00-19:00, Sun 11:00-16:30; best deals are same-day only, www.tkts.co.uk).

**Cheap Tricks:** Most theaters offer discounted tickets, called

London's West End is a mecca for theater buffs.

"concessions," or "concs." These can be for matinee performances, standing-room, restricted-view seats (behind a pillar), senior/student deals, or tickets returned at the last minute. Buying from scalpers on the street can, like anywhere, get you a good deal or a worthless forgery. Many theaters are so small that there's hardly a bad seat. Bold theatergoers buy cheap tickets, then—as the lights begin to dim—scoot up to a better seat. You wouldn't be the only one rustling in the dark. Shakespeare did it.

**Shakespeare's Globe:** The Globe (on the South Bank) presents plays from late April through early October in a thatched, open-air replica of the Bard's original theater (as well as year-round performances indoors). The £5 "groundling" tickets—standing-room at the foot of the stage—are most fun (box office tel. 020/7401-9919; info tel. 020/7902-1400, www.shakespearesglobe.com, £2.50 booking fee). For more on visiting the Globe, see page 146.

## Other Performances

**Concerts at Historic Churches:** Check for free or cheap classical music offered many weekdays around 13:00 (www.timeout.com/london). Popular venues are St. Bride's Church (Tube: St. Paul's, www.stbrides.com), St. James's at Piccadilly (Tube: Piccadilly, www.sjp.org.uk), and St. Martin-in-the-Fields on Trafalgar Square (Tube: Charing Cross, www.stmartin-in-the-fields.org). St. Martin-in-the-Fields also hosts fine evening concerts by candlelight and Wednesday jazz. Evensong services are held at St. Paul's Cathedral, Westminster Abbey, Southwark Cathedral, and St. Bride's Church.

**Opera and Dance:** Some of the world's best opera is belted out at the prestigious Royal Opera House, near Covent Garden (www.roh.org.uk), and at the London Coliseum near Leicester Square (English

Find bargain tickets in Leicester Square.

Attend a play at Shakespeare's Globe.

National Opera, www.eno.org). The critically acclaimed Royal Ballet—where Margot Fonteyn and Rudolf Nureyev forged their famous partnership—is based at the Royal Opera House (www.roh.org.uk). Sadler's Wells Theatre features international and UK-based dance troupes (Tube: Angel, www.sadlerswells.com).

**Jazz:** Ronnie Scott's is London's oldest, and by far most famous, jazz venue, hosting performances daily (47 Frith Street, Tube: Tottenham Court Road or Leicester Square, www.ronniescotts.co.uk).

## Seasonal London

**Summer Fun:** There are plays under the stars at leafy Regent's Park (Tube: Baker Street, www.openairtheatre.org). Royal Albert Hall hosts "Promenade" classical music concerts, known as "Proms," where peasants can score cheap standing-room tickets (Tube: South Kensington, www.bbc.co.uk/proms).

On the South Bank, stroll the Jubilee Walkway along the Thames, from the London Eye to Tower Bridge, past pubs and cafés, the British Film Institute Southbank cinema (Tube: Waterloo or Embankment, check www.bfi.org.uk for schedules), and Shakespeare's Globe. The Scoop, an outdoor amphitheater next to City Hall and Tower Bridge, hosts outdoor movies, concerts, dance, and theater almost nightly and usually for free (Tube: London Bridge, www.morelondon.com).

**Winter Diversions:** From late November to early January, London is dressed in its Victorian Christmas best. Trafalgar Square erects a Christmas tree, and outdoor ice rinks emerge at Somerset House and the Tower of London. Store windows glitter along Oxford Street, Bond Street, Regent Street, and Brompton Road. Father Christmas is in his grotto at the Museum of London (www.museumoflondon.org.uk) and Leicester Square (www.christmasinleicestersquare.com). Hyde Park stages a kitschy carnival (www.hydeparkwinterwonderland.com). Take in a family-fun holiday play called a "panto," or pantomime (try www.hackneyempire.co.uk or www.lwtheatres.co.uk). On the South Bank, nibble your way through Christmas markets at the Borough Market (Tube: London Bridge) or the Southbank Centre Winter Market (Tube: Waterloo, www.southbankcentre.co.uk). Finally, join thousands of revelers on Trafalgar Square to watch fireworks from the London Eye to ring in the New Year.

# Sleeping

London is expensive for lodging. Cheaper rooms are relatively dumpy. I look for places that are clean, central, friendly, quiet, offer good value, and are small enough to have a hands-on owner and stable staff. Four of these six virtues means it's a keeper. Most of all, I emphasize location—my recommended accommodations are in safe, pleasant neighborhoods convenient to sightseeing.

The **Victoria Station** neighborhood (near Big Ben and Buckingham Palace) is central as can be. The area is safe, tidy, and full of decent eateries, and most hotels are a five-minute walk from Tube, bus, and train stations. **South Kensington** (west of Big Ben) is quiet, classy, and upscale; **Earl's Court** has a stately residential feel and several quality chain hotels. **Bayswater** (north of Hyde Park) is a better value than most areas, though can feel a bit sterile, and **North London** has some of my most expensive listings, but is close to the city center.

# London's Hotel Neighborhoods

(Map showing: BAYSWATER/NOTTING HILL, Regent's Park, BRITISH MUSEUM, NORTH LONDON, Hyde Park, WEST END, TRAFALGAR SQUARE, CENTRAL LONDON, ST. PAUL'S, THE CITY, TOWER OF LONDON, WEST LONDON, BUCKINGHAM PALACE, SOUTH KENSINGTON, VICTORIA STATION, WESTMINSTER, EARL'S COURT, THE TUBE'S CIRCLE LINE, BIG BEN, SOUTH BANK, LONDON EYE, Thames River, Hotel Neighborhoods)

## London Hotels

You'll find big, Old World-elegant hotels with modern amenities, as well as familiar-feeling business-class and boutique hotels no different from what you might experience at home. But you'll also find hotels that are more uniquely European. You can expect to book a moderate (if not fancy) double for £100-120, including tax. In pricey London, it's worth looking for deals at chain hotels.

Hotels and B&Bs are sometimes located on the higher floors of a multipurpose building with a secured door. In that case, look for your hotel's name on the buttons by the main entrance. When you ring the bell, you'll be buzzed in.

Hotel elevators are common, though some older buildings still lack them. You may have to climb a flight of stairs to reach the elevator (if so, you can ask the front desk for help carrying your bags up). Elevators are typically very small—pack light, or you may need to send your bags up without you. Air-conditioning isn't a given (I've noted which of my listings have it), but most places have fans.

Most hotels offer an optional breakfast buffet for about £15-20 per person, though it's often not included in their quoted rates (you can choose whether to add breakfast when booking).

## Sleep Code

Dollar signs reflect average rates for a standard double room with breakfast in high season.

| | | |
|---|---|---|
| **$$$$** | **Splurge:** | Most rooms over £160 |
| **$$$** | **Pricier:** | £120-160 |
| **$$** | **Moderate:** | £80-120 |
| **$** | **Budget:** | £40-80 |
| **¢** | **Backpacker:** | Under £40 |
| **RS%** | **Rick Steves discount** | |

Unless otherwise noted, credit cards are accepted and free Wi-Fi is available. If the listing includes RS%, request a Rick Steves discount.

## Making Reservations

Reserve your rooms as soon as you've pinned down your travel dates. Book your room directly via email or phone, or through the hotel's official website. The hotelier wants to know:

- Type(s) of rooms you want and size of your party
- Number of nights you'll stay
- Your arrival and departure dates, written European-style as day/month/year (18/06/21 or 18 June 2021)
- Special requests (en suite bathroom, cheapest room, twin beds vs. double bed, quiet room)
- Applicable discounts (such as a Rick Steves reader discount, cash discount, or promotional rate)

Most places will request a credit-card number to hold your room. If the hotel's website doesn't have a secure form where you can enter the number directly, it's best to share that confidential info via a phone call. If you must cancel, it's courteous—and smart—to do so with as much notice as possible. Cancellation policies can be strict; read the fine print.

Always call or email to reconfirm your reservation a few days in advance. For B&Bs or very small hotels, I call again on my day of arrival to tell my host what time to expect me (especially if arriving after 17:00).

## Budget Tips

If you're on a tight budget, consider the following alternatives to staying at a big, independently run hotel or guesthouse.

**Chain Hotels:** While lacking a personal touch, these at least come with some predictability. But not all chain hotels are created equal—narrow down your search by figuring out which chains suit your tastes (see "Big, Good-Value, Modern Hotels," later), identify the neighborhoods you're interested in, then read reviews on hotel-booking websites (I like Booking.com). Also check auction-type sites (such as Priceline and Hotwire), which match flexible travelers with empty hotel rooms, often at prices well below the hotel's normal rates (generally during quieter times). Note that most chain hotels don't include breakfast in their rates, but will often throw it in for free (or at a discount) if you book direct and ask about it.

**Apartment Rentals:** By booking a room or apartment (through Airbnb or similar site), you'll typically get more space and amenities while paying less than you would at a hotel. And you'll often get to stay in a more local-feeling building and neighborhood. While it's worth looking for places in the areas that appeal to you, keep an open mind. The farther from the city center you're willing to stay, the better the value. (I'd rather sleep in a palatial apartment a 20-minute Tube ride from downtown than pay the same for a grubby budget hotel a five-minute ride away.)

For more options for sleeping (relatively) cheap in London, browse these accommodation discount sites: www.londontown.com (an informative site with a discount booking service), www.athomeinlondon. co.uk and www.londonbb.com (both list central B&Bs), www. lastminute.com, www.visitlondon.com, and www.eurocheapo.com.

## VICTORIA STATION NEIGHBORHOOD

Central, safe, tidy, and full of decent eateries; close to Victoria Tube, bus, and train stations.

**$$$$ Lime Tree Hotel** Stylish and comfortable, thoughtfully decorated rooms, helpful staff, garden in back.

*135 Ebury Street, tel. 020/7730-8191, www.limetreehotel.co.uk*

**$$$ B&B Belgravia** Bright, larger-than-average, good-value rooms, family rooms.

*66 Ebury Street, tel. 020/7259-8570, www.bb-belgravia.com*

**$$$ Luna Simone Hotel** Spacious rooms, modern bathrooms, family run, RS%, family rooms.

*47 Belgrave Road, tel. 020/7834-5897, www.lunasimonehotel.com*

**$$ Best Western Victoria Palace** Business-class comfort, two buildings, elevator in main building only, air-con.

*17 Belgrave Road and 1 Warwick Way, tel. 020/7821-7113, www.bestwesternvictoriapalace.co.uk*

**$ Cherry Court Hotel** Family run, small but bright rooms, central location, great budget choice, family rooms, air-con, laundry.

*23 Hugh Street, tel. 020/7828-2840, www.cherrycourthotel.co.uk*

**$$ OYO Hotels** For very tight budgets, OYO has several very basic options (www.oyorooms.com/gb). One of these is Bakers Hotel, with brightly painted rooms, cheaper single rooms with shared bath, family rooms.

*126 Warwick Way, tel. 020/7834-0729, www.bakershotel.co.uk*

## SOUTH KENSINGTON

Quiet, classy, and upscale; conveniently located on Circle/District and Piccadilly Tube lines.

**$$$$ Aster House** Friendly owners, stately and sedate, comfy rooms, cheerful lobby, lounge, RS%, air-con.

*3 Sumner Place, tel. 020/7581-5888, www.asterhouse.com*

**$$$$ Number Sixteen** Over-the-top class, labyrinthine building, boldly modern decor, plush lounges, tranquil garden, air-con, elevator.

*16 Sumner Place, tel. 020/7589-5232, US tel. 1-888-559-5508, www.numbersixteenhotel.co.uk*

**$$$$ The Pelham Hotel** Business-class hotel, pricey mix of pretense and style, pleasant drawing room, library, air-con, elevator, fitness room.

*15 Cromwell Place, tel. 020/7589-8288, US tel. 1-888-757-5587, www.pelhamhotel.co.uk*

## NEAR EARL'S COURT

Local-feeling and accessible, many high-capacity, relatively expensive hotels on Piccadilly and Circle/District Tube lines.

**$$$$ K+K Hotel George** Grand Georgian building on quiet street, well-appointed rooms, spacious public areas, wellness center, air-con, elevator.

*1 Templeton Place, tel. 020/7598-8700, www.kkhotels.com*

**$$$$ NH London Kensington** Business-style comfort and class, pleasant garden patio, fitness center, extensive optional breakfast buffet, air-con, elevator.

*202 Cromwell Road, tel. 020/7244-1441, www.nh-hotels.com*

**$$$$ Nadler Kensington** On residential block, smallish rooms with kitchenettes, air-con, elevator.

*25 Courtfield Gardens, tel. 020/7244-2255, www.thenadler.com*

**$$$ Henley House Hotel** Warmly run, modern, red-and-black color scheme, handsome brick townhouse, RS%, air-con, elevator.

*30 Barkston Gardens, tel. 020/7370-4111, www.henleyhousehotel.com*

## BAYSWATER, NOTTING HILL, AND NEARBY

Good-value, reasonably priced accommodations in sleepy and very "homely" (Brit-speak for cozy) area on Central Tube line.

**$$$ Vancouver Studios** Modern, tastefully furnished rooms, kitchenettes.

*30 Prince's Square, tel. 020/7243-1270, www.vancouverstudios.co.uk*

**$$$ Phoenix Hotel** Stately public spaces, modern-feeling rooms, elevator.

*1 Kensington Gardens Square, tel. 020/7229-2494, www.phoenixhotel.co.uk*

**$$$ London House Hotel** Modern cookie-cutter rooms at reasonable prices, family rooms, air-con, elevator.

*81 Kensington Gardens Square, tel. 020/7243-1810, www.londonhousehotels.com*

**$$$ Princes Square Guest Accommodation** Businesslike rooms, modern decor, great location, good value, elevator.

*23 Prince's Square, tel. 020/7229-9876, www.princessquarehotel.co.uk*

**$$$ Garden Court Hotel** Understated, homey-but-tasteful rooms, family rooms, elevator.

*30 Kensington Gardens Square, tel. 020/7229-2553, www.gardencourthotel.co.uk*

**$$ Kensington Gardens Hotel** Same owners as Phoenix Hotel, breakfast served at Phoenix Hotel.

*9 Kensington Gardens Square, tel. 020/7243-7600, www.kensingtongardenshotel.co.uk*

**$$$$ Portobello Hotel** On a quiet residential street in Notting Hill, funky yet elegant rooms, elevator.

*22 Stanley Gardens, tel. 020/7727-2777, www.portobellohotel.com*

## NORTH LONDON

Close to the center of London, elegant aura but hordes of tourists. North of Regent Street, a long walk or quick Tube or bus ride from Soho or Hyde Park.

**$$$$ The Sumner Hotel** Large contemporary rooms, fancy lounge, great location, RS%, air-con, elevator.

*54 Upper Berkeley Street, tel. 020/7723-2244, www.thesumner.com*

**$$$$ Charlotte Street Hotel** Inviting public spaces, elegant rooms, connecting family rooms, air-con, elevator.

*15 Charlotte Street, tel. 020/7806-2000, www.charlottestreethotel.com*

**$$$$ The Mandeville Hotel** Genteel British vibe, tasteful art, a worthy splurge, air-con, elevator.

*Mandeville Place, tel. 020/7935-5599, www.mandeville.co.uk*

**$$$ The 22 York Street B&B** Casual, inviting lounge, 10 traditional, comfortable rooms.

*22 York Street—no sign, just look for #22; tel. 020/7224-2990, www.22yorkstreet.co.uk*

### BIG, GOOD-VALUE, MODERN HOTELS

Chain hotels offer modern comforts with no frills. Quality can vary wildly, so check online reviews.

**$$ Motel One** German chain hotel, 10-minute walk from Tower of London.

*24 Minories, tel. 020/7481-6420, www.motel-one.com*

**$$ Premier Inn** Convenient locations include London County Hall (next to the London Eye), at Southwark/Borough Market (near Shakespeare's Globe, 34 Park Street), Southwark/Tate Modern (15 Great Suffolk Street), Kensington/Earl's Court (11 Knaresborough Place), Victoria (82 Eccleston Square), and Leicester Square (1 Leicester Place). In North London, the following branches cluster between King's Cross St. Pancras and the British Museum: King's Cross, St. Pancras, and Euston.

*www.premierinn.com*

**$$ Travelodge** Locations include King's Cross (Gray's Inn Road) and Euston (1 Grafton Place).

*www.travelodge.co.uk*

**$$ Ibis** Locations convenient to London's center include London Blackfriars (49 Blackfriars Road) and London City Shoreditch (5 Commercial Street). The more design-focused Ibis Styles has branches near Earl's Court (15 Hogarth Road) and Southwark, with a theater theme.

*https://ibis.accorhotels.com*

**$ EasyHotel** Tiny rooms, low rates but expensive add-ons (TV, Wi-Fi, bag storage, etc.). Locations include Victoria (34 Belgrave Road), South Kensington (14 Lexham Gardens), and Paddington (10 Norfolk Place).

*www.easyhotel.com*

**$ Hub by Premier Inn** Extremely small rooms (just bigger than the bed) in convenient locations for low prices.

*www.premierinn.com/gb/en/hub.html*

# Eating

London is one of Europe's great food cities, with a cuisine scene that is lively, trendy, and enjoyably diverse. You could try a different cuisine for each meal and never eat "local" English food.

I've listed places by neighborhood—handy to your sightseeing and recommended hotels. (See the restaurant maps on pages 188-191.) Because London can be expensive, I list a wide variety of eateries, from candlelit splurges to take-away fish-and-chips, with an emphasis on fun, moderately priced options.

Whether it's dining well with the upper crust, sharing hearty pub fare with the blokes, or joining young professionals for street food at a market, eating out has become an essential part of the London experience.

## Restaurant Code

Dollar signs reflect the cost of a typical main course.

**$$$$** **Splurge:** Most main courses over £20
**$$$** **Pricier:** £15-20
**$$** **Moderate:** £10-15
**$** **Budget:** Under £10

Carryout fish-and-chips and other takeout food is **$**; a basic pub or sit-down eatery is **$$**; a gastropub or casual but more upscale restaurant is **$$$**; and a swanky splurge is **$$$$**.

### When in London...

Traditionally, Brits have started their day with a large bacon-and-eggs breakfast. Nowadays most Londoners eat lighter, but most hotels still serve the traditional "fry-up," which tides many tourists over until dinner.

Lunch (12:00-14:00) is usually quick and simple—gobbling a pre-made sandwich while perched on a deli stool. Around 16:00, some Londoners still pause for the traditional tea and pastry break. After work, office drones pack London's pubs for an hour of power-drinking and noshing before the commute home. In the early evening, ethnic eateries buzz with the pre-theater crowd. After 19:00, the sit-down restaurants fill up with diners enjoying a romantic meal. Late at night, Londoners relax in the pubs for a pint, a chat, and a game of darts.

### Restaurants

Traditional English fare is still served in classy, wood-paneled restaurants, but you'll find many more establishments featuring foods from around the world. All of Britain's eateries, including pubs that serve food, are now smoke-free. Get the latest on the ever-changing eating scene from weekly entertainment magazines (sold at newsstands), www.london-eating.co.uk, or www.squaremeal.co.uk.

London restaurants can be expensive when ordering à la carte. But portions are generally huge, and sharing is common. Couples could split a single main dish, a salad, and two drinks to make a filling meal.

Take advantage of fixed-price meals and specials for lunch and early-bird dinners. Free tap water is always available.

Though fewer Brits these days make a big deal out of the midafternoon tea-and-biscuit break, many fancy restaurants and hotels offer this genteel tradition. You'll get a pot of tea with scones, jam, clotted (buttery) cream, and finger sandwiches, served in elegant, pinkie-waving surroundings. The cheapest "tea" on the menu is usually a small-assortment "cream tea"; pricier "high tea" is almost a small dinner. Some
places serve tea all afternoon (12:00-18:30), some only from around 15:00 to 17:00. Most welcome tourists in jeans and sneakers (and cost, on average, between £35 and £50). Some of my favorite places include:

**$$$ The Wolseley** serves a good afternoon tea between their meal service. Split one with your companion and enjoy two light meals at a great price in classic elegance (generally served 15:00-18:30 daily, 160 Piccadilly, tel. 020/7499-6996, www.thewolseley.com).

**$$$$ The Capital Hotel,** a luxury hotel near Harrods, has an intimate five-table tearoom (daily 14:00-17:30, book ahead—especially on weekends, 22 Basil Street, Tube: Knightsbridge, tel. 020/7591-1202, www.capitalhotel.co.uk).

**$$$$ Fortnum & Mason** offers a reasonably priced "Take Tea in the Parlour" experience. Or you can indulge in their Diamond Jubilee Tea Salon at royal prices (Mon-Sat 12:00-19:00, Sun until 18:00, reserve at least a week in advance, no shorts, 181 Piccadilly, tel. 020/7734-8040, www.fortnumandmason.com).

**$$$$ Brown's Hotel** serves a fancy afternoon tea in a tearoom that's more contemporary-cozy than pinkie-raising classy (daily 12:00-18:00, reservations smart, no casual clothing, 33 Albemarle Street, Tube: Green Park, tel. 020/7518-4155, www.roccofortehotels.com).

**$$$$ The Orangery at Kensington Palace** may be closed for restoration when you visit. If so, take tea next door at Kensington Palace Pavilion (daily 12:00-16:00, 10-minute walk from either Queensway or High Street Kensington Tube stations, tel. 020/3166-6113, www.hrp.org.uk).

Pubs offer food, drink, and conversation.     Eating global food is "going local" here.

**Service:** Virtually all London restaurants with table service automatically add a 12.5 percent service charge. No additional tip is necessary—locate this charge on your bill before paying to avoid double tipping.

## Pub Grub

Your best bet for good, reasonably priced food is always the corner pub. Many of London's 7,000 pubs serve hearty lunches (roughly 12:00-14:00) and dinners (18:00-20:00) in friendly surroundings under ancient timbers for around £8-15. Standard items are fish-and-chips, "bangers and mash" (sausages and mashed potatoes), and meat pies. But many pubs now also have salad bars, quiche, hamburgers, "jacket potatoes" (baked potato with toppings), pasta, and curried dishes.

You generally order food at the bar—just ask the bartender, who can explain their pub's system. Don't tip unless the place has full table service. Not all pubs serve meals, so look for pubs that proudly advertise their daily specials. For more pub grub listings, including upscale gastropubs (£12-20 meals), try www.thegoodpubguide.co.uk.

Though hours vary, pubs generally serve beer daily from 11:00 to 23:00, though many are open later, particularly on Friday and Saturday. Order your beer or other beverage at the bar and pay as you go, with no need to tip.

The pub is the heart of the people's England. Whether you're a teetotaler or a total beer-guzzler, they should be a part of your travel here. "Pub" is short for "public house." It's an extended living room. Get vocal with a local. Eat, drink, get out of the rain, and watch a soccer match. A cup of darts is free for the asking. Make a few friends and memories, and feel the pulse of London. Cheers!

## Other Budget Alternatives

**Chain Restaurants:** Budget eating in London often means a modern, super-efficient chain restaurant—available in countless varieties, from burgers (Byron) and sushi (Yo!, Wasabi, and Itsu) to Indian (Masala Zone), Thai (Thai Square, Busaba Eathai), and more (Côte Brasserie, Ask, Pizza Express, Wagamama, Eat, and Loch Fyne).

**Street Markets:** London thrives with street markets—the perfect antidote to high prices and interchangeable chain restaurants. Some to try: **Portobello Road Market** in Notting Hill (www.portobelloroad. co.uk), **Borough Market** in Southwark (www.boroughmarket.org.uk), **Southbank Centre Food Market** near the London Eye (closed Tue-Thu, www.southbankcentre.co.uk), and **Camden Lock Market** in North London (www.camdenmarket.com).

**Picnics:** You can easily get prepared food to go. The modern chain eateries on nearly every corner often have simple seating but are designed for takeout. Bakeries serve fresh sandwiches and pasties (savory meat pastries). The corner grocery store has fruit, drinks, fresh bread, tasty British cheese, meat, and local specialties. Supermarkets often have good deli sections, even offering Indian dishes, and sometimes salad bars. Department stores such as Marks & Spencer and even posh Harrods have food halls with carryout options. Decent packaged sandwiches (£3-4) are sold everywhere. Munch a relaxed "meal on wheels" picnic during your open-top bus tour or river cruise.

**Global Cuisine:** Foods from around the world—often from Britain's former colonies—add spice to Britain's cuisine scene. Eating Indian, Bangladeshi, Chinese, or Thai is cheap (even cheaper if you do takeout). Middle Eastern shops sell gyro sandwiches, falafel, and shawarma (grilled meat in pita bread). An Indian samosa (greasy, flaky meat-and-vegetable turnover) costs about £2 and makes a very cheap, if small, meal.

## Some English Specialties

England's oft-maligned "cuisine" focuses on meat, potatoes, and dairy. At breakfast, sample interesting side dishes served with the bacon-and-eggs "fry-up"—grilled tomato, sautéed mushrooms, or baked beans. For lunch, try various meat pies such as steak-and-kidney or shepherd's (lamb) pie. For a full-blown dinner, enjoy roast beef with Yorkshire pudding (which is a pastry, not a pudding).

Desserts, or "sweets," include a variety of sponge cakes and

Desserts—care for some spotted dick?

All hail English ale. Cheers!

"puddings" (breads) slathered in cream, custard, jam, or liqueur. Many come with colorful names like fool, trifle, castle pudding, or spotted dick. Scones are popular.

Beer is a national institution. Always order on tap, not bottled, preferably from the long-handled taps, indicating it comes from casks, not kegs. The British specialty is their amber-colored ales, served warmer and less carbonated than American- and German-style lagers. Most pubs offer a variety of ales, lagers, stouts (dark, like the Irish-made Guinness), ciders (strong taste and kick), and bitters (hop-flavored ales, perhaps the most typical British beer).

Many pubs also have a good selection of wines by the glass and a fully stocked bar for the gentleman's "G and T" (gin and tonic). Pimm's is a refreshing and fruity summer liqueur, traditionally popular during Wimbledon.

Peruse Harrods department store's Fresh Market Hall for grab-and-go picnic items.

## CENTRAL LONDON—NEAR SOHO AND CHINATOWN

Soho is a foodie mecca. These places are convenient to sightseeing and theaters.
Tube: Piccadilly Circus, Leicester Square (see map, page 188)

**1** **$$$ Andrew Edmunds Restaurant** Tiny candlelit local find, European menu, request ground floor, reservations smart (daily 12:30-15:30 & 17:30-22:45).

*46 Lexington Street, tel. 020/7437-5708, www.andrewedmunds.com*

**2** **$$ Mildred's Vegetarian Restaurant** Creative, fun menu, vegan options, happy diners (daily 12:00-23:00).

*45 Lexington Street, tel. 020/7494-1634*

**3** **$$$ Bao** Popular minimalist Taiwanese spot specializing in steamed-bun sandwiches, small portions, arrive early or late (Mon-Sat 12:00-15:00 & 17:30-22:00, Sun 12:00-17:00).

*53 Lexington Street, www.baolondon.com*

**4** **$$$ Temper Soho** Tacos and parathas (Indian-style flatbreads), small but pricey portions, cozy and stylish (Mon-Sat 12:00-22:30, Sun until 21:00).

*25 Broadwick Street, tel. 020/3879-3834*

**5** **$$$ Kiln** Explosive flavors of Northern Thailand, sit with view of wood-fired kilns or in cramped cellar dining room, adventurous menu (daily 12:00-15:00 & 17:00-23:00).

*58 Brewer Street, www.kilnsoho.com*

**6** **$$$ Bocca di Lupo** Stylish and popular, serves half and full portions of classic Italian food, dressy but fun, reservations smart (daily 12:30-15:00 & 17:15-23:00).

*12 Archer Street, tel. 020/7734-2223, www.boccadilupo.com*

**7** **$$$ Kricket Soho** Upmarket Indian fare, a few steps from Piccadilly Circus, stylish main floor with counter seating, dining room in the cellar (Mon-Sat 12:00-14:30 & 17:15-22:30, closed Sun).

*12 Denman Street, tel. 020/7734-5612, www.kricket.co.uk*

**8** **$$$$ Nopi** Run by celebrity chef Yotam Ottolenghi, cellar has communal tables, masterful Eastern Mediterranean cuisine, emphasis on seasonal produce, worth a splurge (Mon-Sat 10:00-15:00 & 17:30-22:30, Sun until 16:00).

*21 Warwick Street, tel. 020/7494-9584, www.ottolenghi.co.uk*

**9** **$$ Hoppers** Sri Lankan cuisine, menu comes with a glossary of key terms, for the adventurous, seek the waitstaff's advice (Mon-Sat 12:00-14:30 & 17:30-22:30, closed Sun).

*49 Frith Street, tel. 020/3319-8110, www.hopperslondon.com*

**10** **$$ Princi** Vast, bright, popular Italian deli/bakery, Milanese flair, order at counter—then find space at a long table or get it to go, also has full-service restaurant (daily 8:00-24:00).

*135 Wardour Street, tel. 020/7478-8888*

**⑪ $$ Yalla** Bohemian-chic hole-in-the-wall, high-quality Beirut street food—hummus, baba ghanoush, tabbouleh, and shawarma, cramped and cozy interior, a few outdoor tables (daily 10:00-24:00).

*1 Green's Court—just north of Brewer Street, tel. 020/7287-7663*

**⑫ $$ Fernandez & Wells** Delightfully simple, top-quality cheeses; Spanish, Italian, or French hams with fine bread and oil; quality sandwiches at lunch (generally Mon-Sat 10:00-22:00, Sun until 17:00).

*1 Denmark Street, tel. 020/3302-9799*

**⑬ $$ Four Seasons** Cheap, reliable, traditional Chinese standby.

*12 Gerrard Street, tel. 020/7287-0900; second location at 23 Wardour*

**⑭ $$ Dumplings' Legend** Chinese joint with made-fresh soup dumplings.

*15 Gerrard Street, tel. 020/7494-1200*

**⑮ $$$ XU Teahouse and Restaurant** Retro-feeling interior, genteel tea counter, short, well-curated Taiwanese menu (daily 12:00-23:00).

*30 Rupert Street, tel. 020/3319-8147*

**⑯ $$$ The Palomar** Israeli and Middle Eastern small plates in a cozy atmosphere (daily 12:00-14:30 & 17:30-23:00).

*34 Rupert Street, tel. 020/7439-8777*

**⑰ $$ Y Ming Chinese Restaurant** Dressy, porcelain-blue European decor, helpful service, authentic Northern Chinese cooking (good £15 meal deal offered 12:00-18:00, open Mon-Sat 12:00-23:30, closed Sun).

*35 Greek Street, tel. 020/7734-2721*

**⑱ $ Jen Café** Chinese eatery, homemade dumplings, stools and simple seating, fast service, fun and inexpensive menu, devoted following (Mon-Wed 11:00-20:30, Thu-Sun until 21:30, cash only).

*4 Newport Place, tel. 020/7287-9708*

**⑲ $$$$ The Wolseley** Grand 1920s showroom of long-defunct British car, formal waiters, traditional Austrian and French dishes, elegant, reasonable prices, reservations required (daily 11:30-23:00).

*160 Piccadilly, tel. 020/7499-6996, www.thewolseley.com*

**⑳ $$$ Brasserie Zédel** Former dining hall of old Regent Palace Hotel, boisterous crowd, rich French food, fast service, great for groups, inexpensive *plats du jour*, live jazz after 21:30 (daily 11:30-24:00).

*20 Sherwood Street, tel. 020/7734-4888, www.brasseriezedel.com*

EATING

## CENTRAL LONDON—NEAR COVENT GARDEN

This area bustles with people and touristy eateries, but has a few good choices. Tube: Covent Garden (see map, page 188)

**㉑** **$$$$ Rules Restaurant** Extremely British, classy yet comfortable, plush Edwardian atmosphere, formal service, splurge for classic English dishes (daily 12:00-23:00).

*34 Maiden Lane, tel. 020/7836-5314, www.rules.co.uk*

**㉒** **$$$ Dishoom** London's hotspot for upscale Indian cuisine, line up early (around 17:00) for a seat, reservations possible only until 17:45, simply phenomenal food (daily 8:00-23:00).

*12 Upper St. Martin's Lane, tel. 020/7420-9320, www.dishoom.com*

**㉓** **$$$ Shapur Indian Restaurant** Well-respected place, classic Indian dishes from many regions, small and dressy, good service (Mon-Fri 12:00-14:30 & 17:30-23:30, Sat 15:00-23:30, closed Sun).

*149 Strand, tel. 020/7836-3730*

**㉔** **$$ Lamb and Flag Pub** Traditional grub since 1772, ground floor for drinking, food service upstairs (long hours daily).

*33 Rose Street, up narrow alley from Floral Street, tel. 020/7497-9504*

## CENTRAL LONDON—NEAR TRAFALGAR SQUARE

Several good choices cluster east of the National Gallery. Tube: Charing Cross (see map, page 188)

**㉕** **$$$ Terroirs Wine Bar** Casual but classy, menu designed to share, mostly Mediterranean, reservations smart (Mon-Sat 12:00-23:00, small bites only 15:00-17:30, closed Sun).

*5 William IV Street, tel. 020/7036-0660, www.terroirswinebar.com*

**㉖** **$$ St. Martin-in-the-Fields Café in the Crypt** In an ancient crypt; breakfast, lunch, dinner, and afternoon tea; live jazz Wed at 20:00 (generally daily 10:00-19:30).

*Under St. Martin-in-the-Fields, tel. 020/7766-1158, www.stmartin-in-the-fields. org*

**㉗** **$$ The Chandos Pub's Opera Room** Fish-and-chips with locals in upstairs room overlooking Trafalgar Square (kitchen open daily 11:30-21:00, Fri until 18:00).

*29 St. Martin's Lane, tel. 020/7836-1401*

**㉘** **$$ Gordon's Wine Bar** Candlelit 15th-century wine cellar with hot- and cold-dish buffet, passionate about port, often crowded (daily 11:00-22:30).

*47 Villiers Street, entrance around corner to the right, tel. 020/7930-1408*

## AROUND ST. PAUL'S

Some classic historic pubs with good beer and grub cluster around St. Paul's Cathedral. Tube: Blackfriars, Bank, Temple (see map, page 190)

**㉙** **$$ Ye Olde Cheshire Cheese** 1667 tavern, once served pub grub to Dickens, Samuel Johnson, Yeats (open daily).

*145 Fleet Street, tel. 020/7353-6170*

**㉚** **$$ The Black Friar** Great Art Nouveau decor (c. 1900-1915), outdoor seating (open daily).

*174 Queen Victoria Street, tel. 020/7236-5474*

**㉛** **$$ The Old Bank of England** Pub in lavish old bank building (closed Sun).

*194 Fleet Street, tel. 020/7430-2255*

**㉜** **$$ The Counting House** Great sandwiches, homemade meat pies, fish, and fresh vegetables; busy after 12:15, especially Thu-Fri (closed Sat-Sun).

*50 Cornhill, tel. 020/7283-7123*

## VICTORIA STATION NEIGHBORHOOD

These places are within a few blocks of Victoria Station. Tube: Victoria (see map, page 191)

**㉝** **$ La Bottega** Upscale Italian deli for fresh pastas, salads, sandwiches; to go or stay (Mon-Fri 7:30-19:00, Sat-Sun 9:00-18:00).

*Corner of Ebury and Eccleston streets, tel. 020/7730-2730*

**㉞** **$$$ The Thomas Cubitt** Trendy gastropub for young professionals, pricey and popular, modern English cooking, reservations smart (daily 12:00-22:00).

*44 Elizabeth Street, tel. 020/7730-6060, www.thethomascubitt.co.uk*

**㉟** **$$ Duke of Wellington** Classic neighborhood pub, forgettable grub, sidewalk seating, inviting interior (Mon-Sat 12:00-15:00 & 18:00-21:00, Sun lunch only).

*63 Eaton Terrace, tel. 020/7730-1782*

**㊱** **$$ Grumbles** Unpretentious, cozy booths, traditional dishes, reservations smart (early-bird specials, open daily 12:00-14:30 & 18:00-23:00).

*35 Churton Street, tel. 020/7834-0149, www.grumblesrestaurant.co.uk*

**㊲** **$ Pimlico Fresh** Breakfast and lunch, organic ingredients, good coffee, fresh-squeezed juices, takeout lunches, vegetarian options (Mon-Fri 7:30-18:00, breakfast until 15:00; Sat-Sun 8:30-18:00).

*86 Wilton Road, tel. 020/7932-0030*

**㊳** **$$$ Seafresh Fish Restaurant** Family-run, classic and creative fish-and-chips, takeaway or eat in (Mon-Sat 12:00-15:00 & 17:00-22:30, closed Sun).

*80 Wilton Road, tel. 020/7828-0747*

**(39)** **$$ The Jugged Hare** Vivid pub scene in old bank building, traditional menu (Mon-Fri 11:00-21:00, Sat-Sun until 20:00).

*172 Vauxhall Bridge Road, tel. 020/7828-1543*

**(40)** **$$ St. George's Tavern** Inviting pub, eat inside or out (daily 12:00-22:00).

*Corner of Hugh Street and Belgrave Road, tel. 020/7630-1116*

**(41)** **$ Tachbrook Market** Delightful, local-feeling food stalls (Mon-Sat 8:00-18:00, closed Sun).

*On Tachbrook Street just off Warwick Way*

## SOUTH KENSINGTON

This upscale area has plenty of colorful restaurants and easy access to shopping and museums. Tube: South Kensington (see map, page 191)

**(42)** **$$ Exhibition Road Eateries** Block-long pedestrian zone lined with enticing eateries including Fernandez & Wells, Thai Square, Comptoir Libanais, and others.

*On Victoria and Albert Museum side of the South Kensington Tube station*

**(43)** **$$$ Daquise** Elevated Polish cuisine, sophisticated but unstuffy, a "destination" restaurant (daily 12:00-23:00).

*20 Thurloe Street, tel. 020/7589-6117*

**(44)** **$$ Moti Mahal** Bangladeshi cuisine, minimalist-yet-upscale ambience, attentive service, try spicy chicken jalfrezi (daily 12:00-14:30 & 17:30-23:30).

*3 Glendower Place, tel. 020/7584-8428*

**(45)** **Old Brompton Road Eateries** Try **$ Bosphorus Kebabs** (Turkish, #59); Beirut Express (Lebanese, #65); or **$$ Rocca** (dressy Italian, #73, daily 11:30-23:30, tel. 020/7225-3413).

**(46)** **$$ The Anglesea Arms** Destination pub with classic feel, good food, crowded bar, mellow dining room (meals served daily 12:00-15:00 & 18:00-22:00).

*15 Selwood Terrace; tel. 020/7373-7960*

**BAYSWATER, NOTTING HILL, AND NEARBY**

These eateries on the northern edge of Kensington Gardens are close to recommended accommodations. Tube: Bayswater, Notting Hill Gate (see map, page 190)

**EATING**

**47** **$$$ Hereford Road** Heavy English cuisine with modern panache, cozy interior, outside tables, reservations smart (daily 18:00-22:00, also open for lunch Thu-Sun 12:00-14:30).

*3 Hereford Road, tel. 020/7727-1144, www.herefordroad.org*

**48** **$$ The Prince Edward** Good grub, family-friendly, upscale-pub setting, sidewalk tables (Mon-Sat 10:30-23:00, Sun 12:00-22:30).

*73 Prince's Square, tel. 020/7727-2221*

**49** **$$$ Geales** Casual interior, delicious crispy battered cod, reservations smart (Tue-Sun 12:00-15:00 & 18:00-22:00, closed Mon).

*2 Farmer Street, tel. 020/7727-7528, www.geales.com*

**50** **$$$$ Mazi** Refined renditions of Greek classics, contemporary, sophisticated, £15 two-course lunch (daily 18:30-22:30, also Tue-Sun 12:00-15:00).

*12 Hillgate Street, tel. 020/7229-3794*

**51** **$ The Fish House of Notting Hill** Old-fashioned, well-loved chippie, takeaway and table service (daily 11:30-22:00).

*29 Pembridge Road, tel. 020/7229-2626*

**52** **$$$$ Maggie Jones's** Solid English cuisine, splittable meat-and-fish pies, bargain prices at lunch, romantic upstairs, lively basement, reservations recommended (daily 12:00-14:00 & 18:00-22:30).

*6 Old Court Place, tel. 020/7937-6462, www.maggie-jones.co.uk*

**53** **$$$$ The Shed** Farm-to-table, rustic-chic setting, hearty portions, reservations smart (Mon-Sat 18:00-24:00, also Tue-Sat 12:00-15:00, closed Sun).

*122 Palace Gardens Terrace, tel. 020/7229-4024, www.theshed-restaurant.com*

**54** **$$ The Churchill Arms Pub and Thai Kitchen** Old-English ambience in front, hearty Thai in back, packed evenings (daily 12:00-22:00).

*119 Kensington Church Street, pub tel. 020/7727-4242, restaurant tel. 020/7792-1246, www.churchillarmskensington.co.uk*

**55** **$ Café Diana** Healthy sandwiches, salads, Middle Eastern food, cash only (daily 8:00-23:00).

*5 Wellington Terrace, tel. 020/7792-9606*

# Central London Restaurants

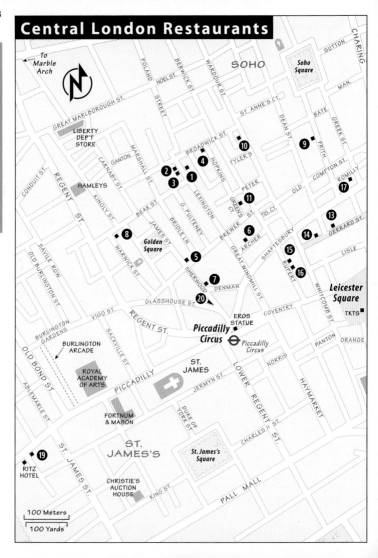

To Marble Arch

SOHO

Soho Square

CHARING

SUTTON

POLAND STREET

NOEL ST.

BERWICK ST.

WARDOUR ST.

MAN.

BATE

DEAN ST.

GREEK ST.

FRITH

GREAT MARLBOROUGH ST.

LIBERTY DEP'T STORE

CARNABY ST.

GANTON ST.

MARSHALL ST.

KINGLY ST.

ST. ANNE'S CT.

BROADWICK ST.

HOPKINS

TYLER'S

PETER

OLD COMPTON ST.

ROMILLY

HAMLEYS

CONDUIT ST.

REGENT ST.

BEAK ST.

JAMES ST.

G. PULTENEY

LEXINGTON

GREEN'S CT.

TIS CT.

SHAFTESBURY

GERRARD ST.

LISLE

WHITCOMB ST.

BRIDLE LN.

BREWER ST.

G. ARCHER

GREAT WINDMILL ST.

RUPERT

Leicester Square

TKTS

Golden Square

WARWICK ST.

SHERWOOD

DENMAN

COVENTRY

PANTON

ORANGE

GLASSHOUSE ST.

EROS STATUE

**Piccadilly Circus**

Piccadilly Circus

SAVILE ROW

OLD BURLINGTON ST.

VIGO ST.

REGENT ST.

SACKVILLE ST.

NORRIS

LOWER REGENT ST.

HAYMARKET

BURLINGTON GARDENS

BURLINGTON ARCADE

ROYAL ACADEMY OF ARTS

PICCADILLY

ST. JAMES

JERMYN ST.

DUKE OF YORK ST.

CHARLES II ST.

OLD BOND ST.

ABLEMARLE ST.

FORTNUM & MASON

ST. JAMES'S

St. James's Square

PALL MALL

RITZ HOTEL

CHRISTIE'S AUCTION HOUSE

KING ST.

100 Meters

100 Yards

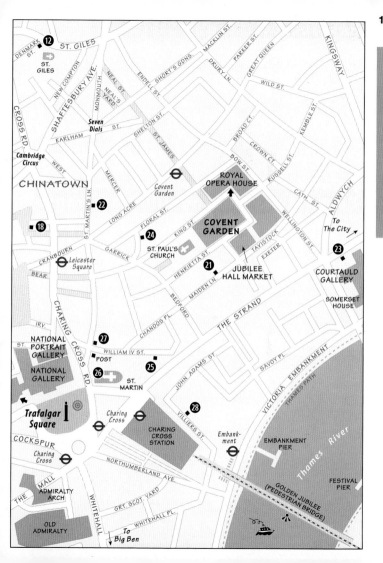

EATING

# Restaurants Around St. Paul's

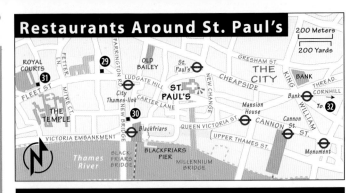

200 Meters
200 Yards

ROYAL COURTS
**31**
FLEET ST
FETTER LN.
MITRE CT.
**29**
FARRINGDON RD.
OLD BAILEY
LUDGATE HILL
St. Paul's
St. Paul's
THE CITY
GRESHAM ST.
KING ST.
CHEAPSIDE
BANK
THREAD.
CORNHILL
Bank
To **32**
THE TEMPLE
City Thameslink
CARTER LANE
NEW CHANGE
ST. PAUL'S
Mansion House
CANNON ST.
William St.
Cannon St. ST.
VICTORIA EMBANKMENT
**30**
New Bridge St.
Blackfriars
QUEEN VICTORIA ST.
UPPER THAMES ST.
Monument
Thames River
BLACKFRIARS BRIDGE
Blackfriars Pier
BLACKFRIARS BRIDGE
MILLENNIUM BRIDGE

# Bayswater & Notting Hill Restaurants

200 Meters
200 Yards

WESTBOURNE GROVE
PEMBRIDGE VILLAS
CHEPSTOW PL.
HEREFORD RD.
Leinster Square
Kensington Gardens Square
POST
**47**
Prince's Square
PORCHESTER GARDENS
QUEENSBOROUGH TERR.
BAYSWATER
**48**
DAWSON PL.
OSSINGTON ST.
ST. PETERSBURGH PL.
Baywater
Moscow Rd.
BARK PL.
Queensway
PORTOBELLO RD.
Pembridge Square
NOTTING HILL
PALACE CT.
Queensway
BAYSWATER RD.
To Marble Arch →
PEMBRIDGE RD.
**51**
KENSINGTON PARK RD.
**55**
Notting Hill Gate
NOTTING HILL GATE
**53**
PLAY-GROUND
BROAD WALK
UXBRIDGE
**49**
KENSINGTON PL.
KENSINGTON CHURCH ST.
PALACE GARDENS TERR.
Kensington Gardens
**50**
CAMPDEN HILL RD.
PEEL ST.
CAMPDEN ST.
BRUNSWICK GDNS.
ORANGERY
Round Pond
**54**
BEDFORD GARDENS
SHEFFIELD TERR.
PALACE GARDENS
HORTON ST.
KENSINGTON PALACE
KENSINGTON
HOLLAND ST.
OLD CT. PL.
**52**
PALACE AVE.
PALACE GREEN
KENSINGTON RD.

EATING

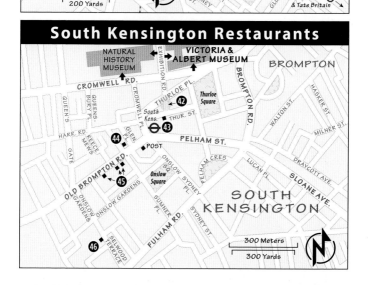

# Victoria Station Neighborhood Restaurants

BELGRAVIA

Eaton Square

LITTLE BEN

Victoria

VICTORIA STATION

WESTMINSTER CATHEDRAL

Chester Square · 33

34 · · 35

POST

VICTORIA COACH STN.

Ebury Square

SHOPS

40

ECCLESTON BRIDGE

Eccleston Square

BELGRAVE

39

38

41

37

36

Warwick Square

PIMLICO RD.

200 Meters
200 Yards

To Pimlico & Tate Britain

# South Kensington Restaurants

NATURAL HISTORY MUSEUM

VICTORIA & ALBERT MUSEUM

BROMPTON

CROMWELL RD.

Thurloe Square

42

South Kens. · 43

44

POST

PELHAM ST.

45

Onslow Square

46

SOUTH KENSINGTON

300 Meters
300 Yards

# Practicalities

# HELPFUL HINTS

## Travel Tips

**Tourist Information:** It's amazing how hard it can be to find unbiased sightseeing information and advice in London. You'll see "Tourist Information" offices advertised everywhere, but most are private agencies that make a big profit selling tours and advance sightseeing and/or theater tickets; others are run by Transport for London (TFL) and are primarily focused on providing public-transit advice.

**The City of London Information Centre,** on the street just below St. Paul's Cathedral, is the only publicly funded—and impartial—"real" TI (Mon-Sat 9:30-17:30, Sun 10:00-16:00; Tube: St. Paul's, tel. 020/7332-1456, www.visitthecity.co.uk).

**Visit London,** which serves the greater London area, doesn't have an office you can visit in person—but does have an information-packed website (www.visitlondon.com).

**"Free" Museums:** Many of London's great museums don't charge admission—though they do suggest a donation (typically £5).

**Advance Tickets:** Buying tickets online in advance is always smart if you don't mind sticking to a schedule. You'll generally save a few pounds per sight and can skip the ticket-buying line once you arrive—though you may need to wait in a security line or pick up your ticket at the sight.

You must book ahead for The Making of Harry Potter: Warner Bros. Studio Tour. For summer, weekends, and holiday periods, consider booking ahead (or risk wasting time in long lines) for the following London sights: Westminster Abbey, the Houses of Parliament, the Churchill War Rooms, St. Paul's Cathedral, the Tower of London, and the London Eye.

**Fast Track Tickets:** To skip the ticket-buying queues at certain London sights, you can buy Fast Track tickets (sometimes called "priority pass" tickets) in advance—and they're typically cheaper than tickets sold right at the sight. These are particularly smart for the Tower of London, The Shard, and Madame Tussauds Waxworks (they're not worth it for the London Eye—you'll still have a wait). They're available at City of London TI, souvenir stands, and faux-TIs scattered throughout touristy areas.

**Time Zones:** Britain is five/eight hours ahead of the East/West

## Helpful Websites

**London Tourist Information:** www.visitthecity.co.uk, www.visitlondon.com
**Britain Tourist Information:** www.visitbritain.com
**Passports and Red Tape:** www.travel.state.gov
**Cheap Flights:** www.kayak.com (for international flights), www.skyscanner.com (for flights within Europe)
**Airplane Carry-On Restrictions:** www.tsa.gov
**Britain Train Schedules:** www.nationalrail.co.uk
**General Travel Tips:** www.ricksteves.com (train travel, rail passes, car rental, travel insurance, packing lists, and much more)

Coasts of the US—and one hour behind most of continental Europe. For a handy time converter, see www.timeanddate.com/worldclock.

**Business Hours:** Most stores are open Monday through Saturday (roughly 9:00 or 10:00 until 17:00 or 18:00), with a late night on Wednesday or Thursday (until 19:00 or 20:00). Department stores are usually open later throughout the week (until about 21:00 Mon-Sat). On Sunday, when stores are closed or have shorter hours, many street markets are lively with shoppers.

**Watt's Up?** Britain's electrical system is 220 volts, instead of North America's 110 volts. Most electronics (laptops, smartphones, cameras) and newer hair dryers convert automatically, so you won't need a converter, but you will need an adapter plug with three square prongs, sold inexpensively at travel stores in the US.

## Safety and Emergencies

**Emergency and Medical Help:** For any emergency service—ambulance, police, or fire—call **112** from a mobile phone or landline. If you get sick, do as the locals do and go to a pharmacy and see a "chemist" (pharmacist) for advice. Or ask at your hotel for help—they'll know of the nearest medical and emergency services.

**Theft or Loss:** To replace a **passport,** you'll need to go in person to an embassy in London (no walk-in passport services; for emergency two-day passport service, schedule an appointment or fill out the online Emergency Passport Contact Form, 24 Grosvenor Square, tel. 020/7499-9000, www.uk.usembassy.gov). If you lose your credit or debit card, report the loss immediately with a collect phone call: Visa (tel. +1 303/967-1096), MasterCard (tel. +1 636/722-7111), and American Express (tel. +1 336/393-1111). For more information, see www. ricksteves.com/help.

## Around Town

**Bookstores:** Stanfords Travel Bookstore stocks a huge selection of travel-related material (Mon-Sat 9:00-20:00, Sun 11:30-18:00, 7 Mercer Walk, Tube: Leicester Square, tel. 020/7836-1321, www. stanfords.co.uk). Waterstones has two locations: on Piccadilly (Mon-Sat 9:00-22:00, Sun 12:00-18:30, café, 203 Piccadilly, tel. 0843-290-8549) and on Trafalgar Square (Mon-Sat 9:00-21:00, Sun 12:00-18:00, tel. 020/7839-4411). Foyles' flagship store is a world of books and literary events (Mon-Sat 9:00-21:00, Sun 11:30-18:00, 107 Charing Cross Road, tel. 020/7437-5660, www.foyles.co.uk).

**Baggage Storage:** Train stations have left-luggage counters, where each bag is scanned (just like at the airport); expect up to 45-minute waits (£12.50/24 hours per item, most stations open daily 7:00-23:00). You can also store bags at the airports (similar rates and hours, www.left-baggage.co.uk).

**Laundry: Pimlico Launderette,** south of Victoria Station, offers self-service and same-day full service (daily 8:00-19:00, last wash at 17:30; 3 Westmoreland Terrace—from Warwick Square, go down Clarendon Street, turn right on Sutherland, and look for the launderette on the left at the end of the street; tel. 020/7821-8692).

# ARRIVAL IN LONDON

## Airports

London has six airports; I've focused my coverage on the two most widely used—Heathrow and Gatwick—with a few tips for using the others.

**Heathrow Airport:** One of the world's busiest airports, Heathrow has four terminals, T-2 through T-5. You can travel between terminals on free trains and buses, but it can be time consuming—plan ahead if you'll need to change terminals (code: LHR, tel. 0844-335-1801, www.heathrow.com).

To get between Heathrow Airport and downtown, you have these options:

***Taxi or Uber:*** Taxis from the airport cost £45-75 to west and central London (one hour). For four people traveling together, this can be a reasonable option. Hotels can often line up a cab back to the airport for about £50. If running, Uber also offers London airport pickup and drop-off.

***Tube:*** The Tube takes you from any Heathrow terminal to downtown London in 50-60 minutes on the Piccadilly Line (6/hour). If you plan to use the Tube for transport in London, it makes sense to buy a pay-as-you-go Oyster card (explained later, under "Getting Around London"); you'll pay a small supplement for the Heathrow-to-London portion.

***Train:*** The **Heathrow Express** goes to Paddington Station (£22-25 one-way, price depends on time of day, £37 round-trip, cheaper if purchased online in advance, covered by BritRail pass; 4/hour, Mon-Sat 5:00-24:00, Sun from 6:00, 15 minutes to downtown from Heathrow Central Station serving T-2/T-3, 21 minutes from T-5; for T-4 take free transfer to Heathrow Central, tel. 0345-600-1515, www.heathrowexpress.co.uk).

***Bus:*** Most buses depart from the outdoor common area called the Central Bus Station, a five-minute walk from T-2/T-3. **National Express** buses go to Victoria Coach Station near the Victoria train/Tube station (£8-10, 1-2/hour, less frequent from Victoria Station to Heathrow, 45-75 minutes depending on time of day, tel. 0871-781-8181, www.nationalexpress.com). A less-frequent National Express bus goes from T-5 directly to Victoria Coach Station.

**Gatwick Airport:** This is London's second-biggest airport (code:

PRACTICALITIES

Heathrow Airport—busy and efficient

From Heathrow to downtown on the Tube

Go with the flow on London's mass transit.
Tourists and locals mingle on the Tube.

LGW, tel. 0844-892-0322, www.gatwickairport.com). **Gatwick Express trains** shuttle conveniently to Victoria Station (£20 one-way, £35 round-trip, at least 10 percent cheaper if purchased online, Oyster cards accepted, 4/hour, 30 minutes, runs 5:00-24:00 daily, a few trains as early as 3:30, tel. 0845-850-1530, www.gatwickexpress.com).

**Other Airports: Stansted** (code: STN, tel. 0844-335-1803, www.stanstedairport.com), **Luton** (LTN, tel. 01582/405-100, www.london-luton.co.uk), **London City** (LCY, tel. 020/7646-0088, www.londoncityairport.com), and **Southend** (SEN, tel. 01702/538-500, www.southendairport.com).

## Trains and Buses

There are nine main train stations, each serving a different region of Britain. You can make reservations and buy tickets for any destination at any train station. For schedules, tickets, and general information on British trains, call 0345-748-4950 or visit www.nationalrail.co.uk. The best all-Europe train schedule information is at www.bahn.de. To see if a rail pass could save you money, check www.ricksteves.com/rail.

**Eurostar:** High-speed trains from St. Pancras International zip you under the English Channel to Paris or Brussels in 2.5 hours and to Amsterdam in 4 hours. Prices can range from less than $100 (second-class, nonrefundable specials) to $450 (first-class full-fare tickets), so do your research and book ahead for the best deals (see www.ricksteves.com/eurostar or www.eurostar.com).

**By Bus—Victoria Coach Station:** For travel beyond London, buses are cheaper—but considerably slower—than the train. Most depart from Victoria Coach Station, a long block south of Victoria Station (Tube: Victoria, www.nationalexpress.com).

# GETTING AROUND LONDON

In London, you're never more than a 10-minute walk from a Tube stop (London's metro/subway). Buses are also convenient, and taxis are everywhere. For more information on routes, tickets, and passes, see www.tfl.gov.uk.

## Tickets and Cards

Paper tickets for the Tube are ridiculously expensive (£5 per Tube ride). Unless you're literally taking only one Tube ride your entire visit, you'll save money (and time) by buying an Oyster card.

Oyster Card: A pay-as-you-go Oyster card allows you to ride the Tube, buses, Docklands Light Railway (DLR), and Overground (mostly suburban trains) for about half the rate of individual tickets. Buy the card at any Tube station ticket machine. You'll pay a refundable £5 deposit and load it with credit. One ride between Zones 1 and 2 during peak time costs £2.90 (£2.40 during off peak). An automatic price cap guarantees you'll never pay more than £7 in one day for rides within Zones 1 and 2. For a three-day visit, get an Oyster card with £20-25 of credit (and top up as needed). To use the card, simply touch it against the yellow card reader at the turnstile or entrance. It flashes green and the fare is automatically deducted. When you exit, tap your card again to "touch out." Note that Oyster cards are not shareable among companions taking the same ride; all travelers need their own.

An Oyster transit pass can save money.

Master London's transit, and go, go, go!

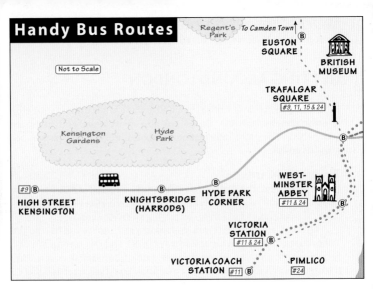

# Handy Bus Routes

(Not to Scale)

Regent's Park • To Camden Town

EUSTON SQUARE ®

BRITISH MUSEUM

TRAFALGAR SQUARE
#9, 11, 15 & 24

®

Kensington Gardens • Hyde Park

®

WEST-MINSTER ABBEY
#11 & 24 ®

#9 ® HIGH STREET KENSINGTON

® KNIGHTSBRIDGE (HARRODS)

® HYDE PARK CORNER

VICTORIA STATION
#11 & 24 ®

VICTORIA COACH STATION #11 ®

PIMLICO #24

**7-Day Travelcard:** For £35.10 (plus a £5 deposit), you get a week's worth of travel in Zones 1-2. It comes as a paper version or can be added to an Oyster card.

## By Tube

The Tube (or Underground—but never "subway") is one of this planet's great people-movers (runs Mon-Sat about 5:00-24:00, Sun about 7:00-23:00).

Get your bearings by studying a map of the system (such as the one in this book's foldout map). Each line has a name (for example, Circle, Northern, or Bakerloo) and two directions (indicated by the end-of-the-line stops). Find the line that will take you to your destination, and figure out roughly which direction (north, south, east, or west) you'll need to go to get there.

At the Tube station, use your Oyster card, Travelcard, or ticket to pass through the turnstile (you'll also need it to exit). Find your train by following signs to your line and the (general) direction it's headed (such as Central Line: Eastbound). Since some tracks are shared by several lines, read signs on the platform to confirm that the

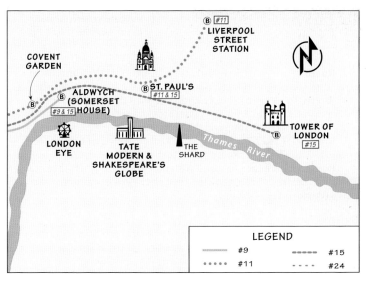

approaching train is going to your specific destination. Upon exiting the system, check maps and signs for the most convenient street exit.

Rush hours (8:00-10:00 and 16:00-19:00) can be packed and sweaty. Be prepared to walk significant distances within Tube stations and ride long escalators (stand on the right to let others pass). Delays are common. A general rule of thumb is that it takes 30 minutes to travel six Tube stops (including walking time within stations). Be wary of thieves, especially amid the jostle of boarding and leaving crowded trains.

## By Bus

London's bus system is excellent. Use it for quick little straight shots, or even just to get to a Tube stop. However, during bump-and-grind rush hours (8:00-10:00 and 16:00-19:00), you'll usually go faster by Tube.

To ride, you must have an Oyster card, a paper Travelcard, or a one-day Bus & Tram Pass (£5, buy on day of travel only—not beforehand, from ticket machine in any Tube station). There are no single-trip tickets, and you can't pay on board. If you're using your Oyster card, any bus ride in downtown London costs £1.50 (capped at £4.50/

day). As you board, touch your Oyster card to the card reader, or show your paper pass to the driver. There's no need to show or tap your card when you hop off.

Here are some of the most useful routes:

**Route #9:** High Street Kensington to Knightsbridge (Harrods) to Hyde Park Corner to Trafalgar Square to Aldwych (Somerset House).

**Route #11:** Victoria Coach Station to Victoria Station (train) to Westminster Abbey to Trafalgar Square to Covent Garden to St. Paul's and Liverpool Street Station and the East End.

**Route #15:** Trafalgar Square to St. Paul's to Tower of London (occasionally with heritage "Routemaster" old-style double-decker buses).

**Route #24:** Pimlico to Victoria Station to Westminster Abbey to Trafalgar Square to Euston Square, then all the way north to Camden Town (Camden Lock Market).

## By Taxi

London is the best taxi town in Europe. Big, black, carefully regulated cabs are everywhere. I've never met a crabby cabbie in London. They love to talk, and they know every nook and cranny in town.

If a cab's top light is on, just wave it down (even if it's going in the other direction), or find the nearest taxi stand. Telephoning a cab costs a little more (tel. 0871-871-8710).

Rides start at £3. Rates go up at night and on weekends. Extra charges are explained in writing on the cab wall. All cabs accept credit and debit cards. Tip a cabbie by rounding up (maximum 10 percent).

A typical daytime trip downtown will cost you about £8-12 (for example, St. Paul's to the Tower of London, or between the two Tate museums). All cabs can carry five passengers, and some take six, for the same cost as a single traveler. So for a short ride, three adults in a cab travel at close to Tube prices. Avoid cabs when traffic is bad—they're slow and expensive, because the meter keeps running even at a standstill.

## By Uber

Uber faces legal challenges in London and may not be operating when you visit. If Uber is running, it can be much cheaper than a taxi and is a handy alternative if there's a long line for a taxi or if no cabs are available. Uber drivers generally don't know the city as well as regular cabbies, and they don't have the access to some fast lanes that taxis do. Still, if you like using Uber, it can work great here.

## Tipping

Tipping in Britain isn't as automatic and generous as it is in the US, but some general guidelines apply.

**Restaurants:** Virtually all London restaurants with table service automatically tack on a 12.5 percent service charge to your bill. No additional tip is necessary—look for this on your bill before paying to avoid double tipping.

**Taxis:** For a typical ride, round up your fare a bit (maximum 10 percent; for instance, if the fare is £7.40, pay £8).

**Services:** In general, if someone in the tourism or service industry does a super job for you, a small tip of a pound or two is appropriate. If you're not sure whether (or how much) to tip, ask a local for advice.

# MONEY

Britain uses the pound sterling. The British pound (£), also called a "quid," is broken into 100 pence (p). Pence means "cents." You'll find coins ranging from 1p to £2 and bills from £5 to £50. (Check www.oanda.com for the latest exchange rates.)

Here's my basic strategy for using money in Great Britain:

Upon arrival, head for a cash machine (ATM) at the airport and withdraw pounds, using a debit card with low international transaction fees. In London, credit cards are widely accepted, even for small purchases (and sometimes the only acceptable form of payment). But having cash on hand still helps you out of a jam if your card randomly doesn't work, and it can be useful to pay for cheap food, tips, and local guides.

US credit cards generally work fine in Europe. Some European card readers will accept your card as-is; others may generate a receipt for you to sign or prompt you to enter your PIN (so it's important to know the code for each of your cards).

At self-service payment machines (transit-ticket kiosks, parking, etc.), results are mixed, as US cards may not work in some unattended transactions. If your card won't work, look for a cashier who can process your card manually—or pay in cash.

# STAYING CONNECTED

## Making International Calls

For the dialing instructions below, use the complete phone number, including the area code (if there is one).

**From a Mobile Phone:** It's easy to dial with a mobile phone. Whether calling from the US to Europe, country to country within Europe, or from Europe to the US—it's all the same: Press zero until you get a + sign, enter the country code (44 for Great Britain), then dial the phone number.

**From a US Landline to Europe:** Dial 011 (US/Canada access code), country code (44 for Great Britain), and phone number.

**From a European Landline to the US or Europe:** Dial 00 (Europe access code), country code (1 for the US), and phone number.

To make a collect call to the US, dial 0800-022-9111. For more phoning help, see www.howtocallabroad.com.

## Budget Tips for Using A Mobile Phone in Europe

**Sign up for an international plan.** To stay connected at a lower cost, sign up for an international service plan through your carrier. Most providers offer a simple bundle that includes calling, messaging, and data.

**Use free Wi-Fi whenever possible.** Unless you have an unlimited-data plan, you're best off saving most of your online tasks for Wi-Fi. Most accommodations in Europe offer free Wi-Fi, and many cafés have free hotspots for customers. You'll also often find Wi-Fi at TIs, city squares, major museums, public-transit hubs, airports, and aboard trains and buses.

**Minimize use of your cellular network.** Even with an international data plan, wait until you're on Wi-Fi to Skype, download apps, stream videos, or do other megabyte-greedy tasks. Using a navigation app such as Google Maps over a cellular network can take lots of data, so do this sparingly or offline.

**Use Wi-Fi calling and messaging apps.** Skype, WhatsApp, FaceTime, and Google Hangouts are great for making free or low-cost calls or sending texts over Wi-Fi worldwide.

# RESOURCES FROM RICK STEVES

**Begin your trip at RickSteves.com:** This guidebook is just one of many titles in my series on European travel. I also produce a public television series, *Rick Steves' Europe,* and a public radio show, *Travel with Rick Steves*. My mobile-friendly website is *the* place to explore Europe in preparation for your trip. You'll find thousands of fun articles, videos, and radio interviews; a wealth of money-saving tips; travel news dispatches; a video library of my travel talks; my travel blog; my latest guidebook updates (www.ricksteves.com/update); and my free Rick Steves Audio Europe app. You can also follow me on Facebook, Instagram, and Twitter.

# Packing Checklist

## Clothing

❑ 5 shirts: long- & short-sleeve
❑ 2 pairs pants (or skirts/capris)
❑ 1 pair shorts
❑ 5 pairs underwear & socks
❑ 1 pair walking shoes
❑ Sweater or warm layer
❑ Rainproof jacket with hood
❑ Tie, scarf, belt, and/or hat
❑ Swimsuit
❑ Sleepwear/loungewear

## Money

❑ Debit card(s)
❑ Credit card(s)
❑ Hard cash (US $100-200)
❑ Money belt

## Documents

❑ Passport
❑ Tickets & confirmations: flights, hotels, trains, rail pass, car rental, sight entries
❑ Driver's license
❑ Student ID, hostel card, etc.
❑ Photocopies of important documents
❑ Insurance details
❑ Guidebooks & maps
❑ Notepad & pen
❑ Journal

## Toiletries Kit

❑ Soap, shampoo, toothbrush, toothpaste, floss, deodorant, sunscreen, brush/comb, etc.
❑ Medicines & vitamins
❑ First-aid kit
❑ Glasses/contacts/sunglasses
❑ Sewing kit
❑ Packet of tissues (for WC)
❑ Earplugs

## Electronics

❑ Mobile phone
❑ Camera & related gear
❑ Tablet/ebook reader/laptop
❑ Headphones/earbuds
❑ Chargers & batteries
❑ Plug adapters

## Miscellaneous

❑ Daypack
❑ Sealable plastic baggies
❑ Laundry supplies
❑ Small umbrella
❑ Travel alarm/watch

## Optional Extras

❑ Second pair of shoes
❑ Travel hairdryer
❑ Water bottle
❑ Fold-up tote bag
❑ Small flashlight & binoculars
❑ Small towel or washcloth
❑ Tiny lock
❑ Extra passport photos

# INDEX

# Start your trip at

## *Our website enhances this book and turns*

## Explore Europe

At ricksteves.com you can browse through thousands of articles, videos, photos and radio interviews, plus find a wealth of money-saving travel tips for planning your dream trip. And with our mobile-friendly website, you can easily access all this great travel information anywhere you go.

## TV Shows

Preview the places you'll visit by watching entire half-hour episodes of *Rick Steves' Europe* (choose from all 100 shows) on-demand, for free.

# ricksteves.com

*your travel dreams into affordable reality*

## Radio Interviews

Enjoy ready access to Rick's vast library of radio interviews covering travel tips and cultural insights that relate specifically to your Europe travel plans.

## Travel Forums

Learn, ask, share! Our online community of savvy travelers is a great resource for first-time travelers to Europe, as well as seasoned pros.

## Travel News

Subscribe to our free Travel News e-newsletter, and get monthly updates from Rick on what's happening in Europe.

## Classroom Europe

Check out our free resource for educators with 400+ short video clips from the *Rick Steves' Europe* TV show.

# Audio Europe™

## Rick's Free Travel App

Get your FREE Rick Steves Audio Europe™ app to enjoy…

- Dozens of self-guided tours of Europe's top museums, sights and historic walks

- Hundreds of tracks filled with cultural insights and sightseeing tips from Rick's radio interviews

- All organized into handy geographic playlists

- For Apple and Android

With Rick whispering in your ear, Europe gets even better.

# Find out more at ricksteves.com

# Pack Light and Right

*Gear up for your next adventure at ricksteves.com*

### Light Luggage

Pack light and right with Rick Steves' affordable, custom-designed rolling carry-on bags, backpacks, day packs and shoulder bags.

### Accessories

From packing cubes to moneybelts and beyond, Rick has personally selected the travel goodies that will help your trip go smoother.

## Shop at ricksteves.com

# Rick Steves has

## *Experience maximum Europe*

### Save time and energy

This guidebook is your independent-travel toolkit. But for all it delivers, it's still up to you to devote the time and energy it takes to manage the preparation and logistics that are essential for a happy trip. If that's a hassle, there's a solution.

### Rick Steves Tours

A Rick Steves tour takes you to Europe's most interesting places with great guides and small groups

# great tours, too!

## *with minimum stress*

of 28 or less. We follow Rick's favorite itineraries, ride in comfy buses, stay in family-run hotels, and bring you intimately close to the Europe you've traveled so far to see. Most importantly, we take away the logistical headaches so you can focus on the fun.

them repeat customers—along with us on four dozen different itineraries, from Ireland to Italy to Athens. Is a Rick Steves tour the right fit for your travel dreams? Find out at ricksteves.com, where you can also request Rick's latest tour catalog.

Europe is best experienced with happy travel partners. We hope you can join us.

### Join the fun

This year we'll take 33,000 free-spirited travelers—nearly half of

# A Guide for Every Trip

## BEST OF GUIDES

*Full-color guides in an easy-to-scan format, focusing on top sights and experiences in popular destinations*

Best of England
Best of Europe
Best of France
Best of Germany

Best of Ireland
Best of Italy
Best of Scotland
Best of Spain

## COMPREHENSIVE GUIDES

*City, country, and regional guides printed on Bible-thin paper. Packed with detailed coverage for a multi-week trip exploring iconic sights and more*

Amsterdam &
  the Netherlands
Barcelona
Belgium: Bruges, Brussels,
  Antwerp & Ghent
Berlin
Budapest
Croatia & Slovenia
Eastern Europe
England
Florence & Tuscany
France
Germany
Great Britain
Greece: Athens &
  the Peloponnese
Iceland

Ireland
Istanbul
Italy
London
Paris
Portugal
Prague & the Czech Republic
Provence & the French
  Riviera
Rome
Scandinavia
Scotland
Sicily
Spain
Switzerland
Venice
Vienna, Salzburg & Tirol

Many guides are available as ebooks.

## POCKET GUIDES
*Compact guides for shorter city trips*

| | | |
|---|---|---|
| Amsterdam | Italy's Cinque Terre | Prague |
| Athens | London | Rome |
| Barcelona | Munich & Salzburg | Venice |
| Florence | Paris | Vienna |

## SNAPSHOT GUIDES
*Focused single-destination coverage*

Basque Country: Spain & France
Copenhagen & the Best of Denmark
Dublin
Dubrovnik
Edinburgh
Hill Towns of Central Italy
Krakow, Warsaw & Gdansk
Lisbon
Loire Valley
Madrid & Toledo
Milan & the Italian Lakes District
Naples & the Amalfi Coast
Nice & the French Riviera
Normandy
Northern Ireland
Norway
Reykjavík
Rothenburg & the Rhine
Sevilla, Granada & Southern Spain
St. Petersburg, Helsinki & Tallinn
Stockholm

## CRUISE PORTS GUIDES
*Reference for cruise ports of call*

Mediterranean Cruise Ports
Scandinavian & Northern European
  Cruise Ports

## TRAVEL SKILLS & CULTURE
*Greater information and insight*

Europe 101
Europe Through the Back Door
Europe's Top 100 Masterpieces
European Christmas
European Easter
European Festivals
For the Love of Europe
Travel as a Political Act

## PHRASE BOOKS & DICTIONARIES

French
French, Italian & German
German
Italian
Portuguese
Spanish

## PLANNING MAPS

Britain, Ireland & London
Europe
France & Paris
Germany, Austria & Switzerland
Iceland
Ireland
Italy
Scotland
Spain & Portugal

# PHOTO CREDITS